The Past Afloat

The Past Afloat

Anthony Burton

Photography by

Clive Coote

André Deutsch
British Broadcasting Corporation

This book is published to accompany
a series of BBC Television Programmes first broadcast
on BBC 2 in Spring 1982

Series producer: Michael Garrod

Published to accompany a series of programmes in consultation
with the BBC Continuing Education Advisory Council

Text © 1982 by Anthony Burton
Photographs © 1982 by the British Broadcasting Corporation
and André Deutsch Limited
First published 1982
Published by the British Broadcasting Corporation
35 Marylebone High Street, London W1M 4AA
and André Deutsch Limited
105 Great Russell Street, London WC1B 3LJ

Printed in England by Jolly and Barber Limited, Rugby
This book is typeset in VIP Palatino, 10pt leaded 2pts

ISBN 0 233 97433 4 (André Deutsch)
ISBN 0 563 16480 8 (BBC)

Contents

7   Introduction

9   Chapter 1
    Shipshape

29 Chapter 2
    Setting Sail

57 Chapter 3
    Sail and Steam

83 Chapter 4
    Full Steam Ahead

107 Chapter 5
    The Silver Darlings

127 Chapter 6
    Wooden Walls

145 Chapter 7
    Ironclad

165 Chapter 8
    Home from the Sea

182 *Gazetteer*

185 *Further Reading*

186 *Glossary*

190 *Index*

Acknowledgement is due to the following for permission to reproduce photographs:

ASHMOLEAN MUSEUM, OXFORD *St Nicholas Rebuking the Tempest* by Bicci di Lorenzo, page 30; BBC HULTON PICTURE LIBRARY Canning Dock and Customs House, Liverpool, page 174; ALAN BINNS N. Ferriby boat, page 13; BRITISH MUSEUM Sutton Hoo, pages 16 and 18, shipbuilding (Roy.15EIV f. 53v), page 20; CROWN COPYRIGHT SCIENCE MUSEUM, bombarding, page 157; T. LEECH *Vic 32*, page 90; R. W. MALSTER *Albion* at Bungay Staithe, page 45; THE MARITIME TRUST *Lydia Eva*, page 116 top; MERSEYSIDE COUNTY MUSEUMS Albert Dock, Liverpool, page 177; NATIONAL MARITIME MUSEUM Graveney boat, page 19, Humber keel, page 31, Thames hay barge, page 53, *Kathleen and May*, page 58, *Cutty Sark*, page 63, *Cutty Sark* at Sydney, page 64, *Comet*, page 71, *Rattler* and *Alecto* tug of war, page 78, *Great Britain*, page 84 top, *Warrior*, page 146; N.E.I. PARSONS LTD *Turbinia*, page 98; R.N.L.I. ZETLAND MUSEUM, RED-CAR *Zetland*, page 125; SCOTTISH FISHERIES MUSEUM, ANSTRUTHER *Reliance*, page 112 top, fleet, page 114; TYNE AND WEAR COUNTY COUNCIL MUSEUMS *Turbinia* at Spithead, page 100.

The Glossary drawings are by Hugh Ribbans

Introduction

This is not a history of ships and shipping, nor even of maritime Britain, but rather an attempt to look at what remains of our maritime past and put it into a historical context. That the result is somewhat uneven, with many gaps in the historical framework, is not because of my own lack of interest in certain areas but because of a regrettable shortage of material. In spite of heroic efforts by the National Maritime Museum, the Maritime Trust and several small preservation groups, much of our maritime past has simply vanished. In a nation with a long and often splendid history of seafaring, this seems to me to be a disgrace. So little remains, and what does remain is too often under threat. Whilst working on this project, doubts were being expressed about the continuation in service of *P.S. Waverley*: the doubts have since faded, but that there should have ever been any question of allowing the world's last seagoing paddle-steamer to disappear from the water is astonishing. The future of this and the other vessels depends ultimately on public support. If this book and the television series which it accompanies do anything to encourage more people to go and see the museums and the boats and ships for themselves, then they will have achieved their main purpose.

Inevitably a project of this sort involves an author in a long list of debts of gratitude. Top of that list is Michael Garrod who, having already produced me in one television series, was foolhardy enough to ask me to do a second. My thanks go to all the television crew for never groaning too loudly at the retakes. I should also like to thank all those who helped with the book, especially Dr McGowan of the National Maritime Museum, who kindly agreed to read the manuscript. Any errors that remain are, however, all my own. And finally, a very large thank you to all the skippers who allowed me on to their boats, and who helped to make work on this project such a delight.

Anthony Burton

1   *Shipshape*

Man is an inventive creature. He has contrived all manner of machines and devices to ease him on his way through life, but, of all these, few can be more beautiful than the sailing boat. No one quite knows when the sailing boat first appeared, but it has been with us for a time that can be measured in millennia rather than centuries, and it is still with us today. All around the coastline of Britain are harbours and marinas crammed with sleekly elegant craft that on a bright summer day will fill the sea with sail. They make a brave sight, but to a sailor coming back from the dead from, say, two centuries ago, they would be utterly mystifying. What is the use of that rich racing yacht? It has no space for cargo, little room for passengers and no role in times of war.

If told it was intended merely for pleasure, our time-traveller would be even more bemused, for the idea of putting to sea for the pure fun of it is a very modern notion. Two centuries ago there was scarcely a boat on the water that was not there to do a job of work, and it was often said that the man who went to sea for pleasure would go to hell for a holiday. Down the years, all the changes that had been made had been moving towards one end – to produce a boat that would be ideal for the particular job it was expected to perform. In this book we shall be concentrating almost exclusively on the working boat and its development rather than on the glossy beauty of the modern yacht. Do not be disheartened: for in the world of boats and ships, beauty and utility are by no means incompatible.

Racing, for example, is not limited to pleasure boats. Each summer a series of races is held around the estuaries of south-east England, carrying on a tradition that was begun in 1863 when Mr Henry Dodd inaugurated the Annual Barge Sailing Matches. These matches were and are for Thames sailing barges and today they form one of the great sailing spectacles of the year. But unlike the dinghy and yacht races that spatter the nautical calendar, they have their origins in the world of work. The barges are now used mainly for pleasure-boating, but when Mr Dodd started his barge matches, he had a serious purpose in mind, They were to act much as the big rallies do for motor manufacturers today: they were to be the testing grounds where new equipment and new designs could be tried and proved. The end product was a vessel that could scarcely be improved upon for the job it was asked to do, and which is still the largest sailing cargo vessel ever to be handled by a two-man crew. Indeed, barge-men take great delight in telling the story of the expert who wanted to use modern technology to improve the old Thames barge. All the factors to be taken into account – loads, crew requirements, waters to be sailed and so on – were fed into a computer. After a good deal of electronic cogitation, the computer eventually produced the ideal vessel: a traditional Thames barge!

Two centuries of design meet at sea: the spritsail barge and the modern coaster

The first cargo-carrying sailing boat appeared on the water literally thousands of years ago, and the history of the sailing barge itself goes back several centuries. Even what might seem at first to be the simplest

9

part of the vessel, the hull, was subject to the same great changes as such self-evidently complex parts of the vessel as sails and rigging.

Any hull is a compromise. Those racing yachts are built entirely for speed, with a hull designed to minimise resistance to water. They are supremely well fitted to their particular job, to provide a basic platform for masts and sails, with the bare minimum of space for the crew. The ideal design for a cargo vessel required to take the maximum possible load would look quite different: it would be an oblong box with every inch of space utilisable and easily reached. Such a vessel would, however, require an enormous effort to shift it through the water – hence the compromise, and a puzzle that has beset boat designers ever since man took to the water. How do you find the right balance between the work the boat has to do and the work that has to be done to the boat, simply in order to move it from place to place? And there are other factors to be considered, of which stability and seaworthiness are by no means the least important. Over the centuries during which the ship hull has changed and evolved, ship designers and ship-wrights have gradually edged closer to that elusive point of balance.

Right. Barges manœuvering for position at the start of the Medway match

Spritsail barges are perhaps the most popular of all preserved craft. Waiting for the start of the Medway barge match

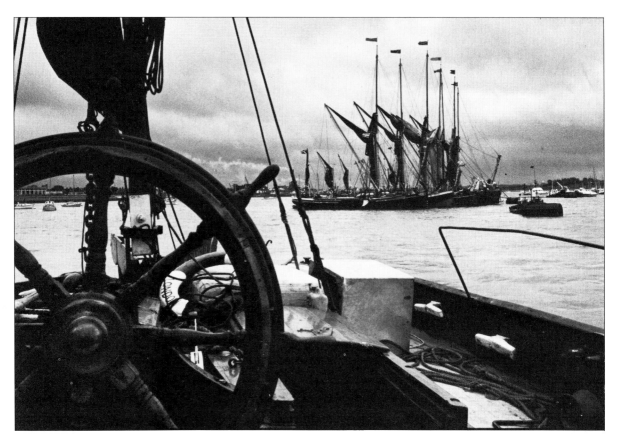

At this stage, one would like to be able to lay out a neat, logical programme, starting with a primitive craft and ending up with something approximating ever more closely to the perfect hull. It is in fact possible to write out such a lovely, logical sequence, but it would have to be based on conjecture, as the evidence is desperately scarce, and we cannot be sure of the true sequence of events. We do have the remains of some early ships for investigation, and we can now, thanks to modern radio carbon techniques, date them with reasonable accuracy, but what we cannot tell is whether the ship we have in front of us was typical of its period or not. It is rather as if a historian of the thirtieth century were to try and study land transport in Britain in our own time, only to find that the records had vanished and all he had to go on were the incomplete remains of a single bicycle. He would know nothing of the internal combustion engine, of railways or a horde of other things. He might be able to guess from later trends that something else was around beside bicycles, but he could never be certain, and he might end up with a very odd picture of twentieth-century life. With just a few vessels surviving from a period of thousands of years, we can tell our evolutionary story, but we have to remember that it could be wildly inaccurate. What follows, then, is an account based on incomplete evidence, but one which seems to fit in best with the little that we do know.

Logic would suggest that the first artificial aids to help man keep afloat and move through the water would be such simple objects as logs. They can be clung to for support, but manœuvring is very difficult. An alternative is to use a less cumbersome float, like a skin filled with air: such devices certainly were used in the ancient world, and can be seen in Assyrian wall sculptures. A second alternative would be to sit or lie on the floating piece of wood – but then, as many an adventurous child has discovered, the phrase 'easy as falling off a log' takes on new significance. Greater stability can be achieved by lashing several logs together to form a raft, but what is gained in stability is lost in manœuvrability. The next stage seems obvious. Hollow out the log: turn your piece of wood into a boat.

Using even the comparatively primitive tools of a stone-age or neolithic culture, it is no difficult task to hollow out the log and plug up the ends with waterproof material. With increased confidence, the boat builder could begin to shape the wood so that it became less a hollow log and more a curved plank, pointing upwards at bow and stern. Such vessels have certainly been discovered in Britain and there is evidence to suggest that they continued in use for an amazingly long period, right up to medieval times. They still suffer from serious disadvantages, particularly lack of stability. This can be overcome by the addition of outriggers, the forerunners of the modern catamarans and other multi-hulled boats. Alternatively, the shaped plank can be treated as a base or keel, and the sides built up around it. And that brings us to our first vessel.

The little village of North Ferriby stands on the northern bank of the Humber, and it was here in the river mud that three ancient ships were located. A less convenient site for archaeological work could scarcely be imagined, for it was regularly covered by the tidal waters of the river – and was somewhat closer to the low-water than to the high-water mark. All three vessels were located by two brothers, E. V. and C. W. Wright, the former being responsible for the major part of the excavation. The Wrights found the first boat in 1938, at a spot where the shifting silt had shown traces of a vessel as early as the 1880s. Once the brothers had located the remains, they set out to record and save as much as they could. With the help of a few friends they began digging, recording and refilling, in the five-hour stretches allowed them at low tide. Time was against them in other ways, too, for war was close, and they had to be content with removing three sections which were in danger of being washed away. These were stored in the family's suitably damp greenhouse.

E. V. Wright went to war, but on leave in 1940 he returned to the site, and it was then that he discovered boat number two. This time, working single-handed, he was able to clear the two ends of the vessel. Later, on a second leave, he uncovered a central section and that, frustratingly, had to be that until he returned to civilian life in 1946. He invited Charles Phillips, who had directed the excavation of the Saxon burial ship at Sutton Hoo in 1939, to come up to Humberside to see his ships. Phillips was impressed, sufficiently so to persuade

The third of the North Ferriby boats emerging from the mud of the Humber

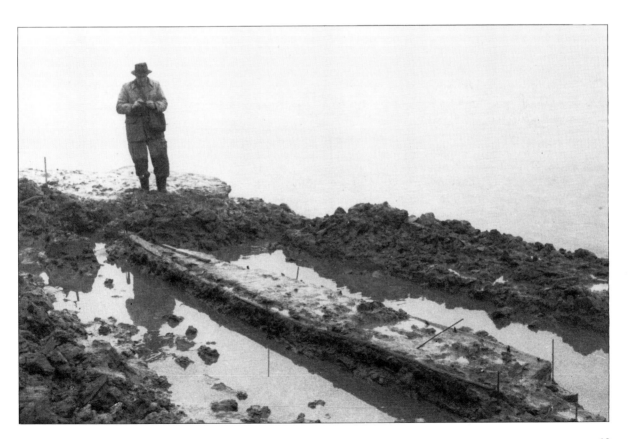

the British Museum and the National Maritime Museum to mount a rescue operation to lift the ships from their wet and muddy graves.

Work began in the late summer of 1946. The obstacles were formidable. In the limited time available at each tide, those involved had to work at full speed while struggling with the cloying mud. They spent three weeks attempting to lift boat number one. Their idea was to slice through the clay beneath the vessel, slide a cradle made up of quarter-inch boiler plates underneath and then drag the whole thing up above the high-water mark, where work could continue at a less frantic pace. Preparation went well, but when it came to the final stage there was nearly a total disaster. The boat collapsed and the fragments had to be collected up before the tide engulfed them. They were carried to safety and laid out like a huge jigsaw, every scrap carefully numbered and given its appointed place in the overall plan of the vessel. It was decided not to risk a repeat performance with number two; instead, they cut it into manageable pieces and hauled it up the bank. The next problem was that of stabilising and preserving the sodden wood – and again there were mixed results. After years of work by the scientists, the pieces of number two were saved, but number one suffered a less happy fate and very little of it now remains. At least it had been carefully recorded.

So to boat number three, discovered on the same site in 1963. Again an attempt was made to lift the vessel whole, again the attempt failed – and again the excavators were left with a jigsaw ship. This time, however, they had the advantage of being able to use new research into the techniques of preservation, and the parts were carefully and successfully treated by the archaeologists of the National Maritime Museum, Greenwich.

Today, the muddy banks of the Humber show no signs of either ancient ships or excavation. Thanks, however, to a splendid and imaginative reconstruction in the Greenwich museum, we do at least have a very good idea of what the site looked like when work was in progress on the first of the boats. It also gives an indication of just what sort of boat it was, while thanks to the notes and careful drawings made at the time, we can see quite accurately how and when this particular ship was constructed. The first and most important question to be answered is that of age. The ships were clearly ancient, and associated finds and radio carbon-dating have enabled scientists to place the North Ferriby boats in the Bronze Age, somewhere around 1500 BC. So, how did our ancestors of over three thousand years ago set about building a ship that could carry passengers or cargo on the broad waters of the Humber?

The most impressive feature is the size – a massive $43\frac{1}{2}$ feet long. The keel (the base of the ship) is made up of two planks, carved from solid oak with an upward curve at either end, and scarfed together at the centre of the boat. On this base, sides were built up, formed by somewhat thinner planks. Considerable ingenuity was shown in the construction: no nails were employed, the planks being sewn together by strips of yew. The actual joints between the planks were like a kind of tongue and groove, and were made watertight by packing with moss and covering with slats. The keel was extended upwards by two side-planks or strakes, and cleats were found on the keel, which had originally held cross-battens to strengthen the floor. Examination of tool-marks on the wood suggests that at least two types of implement were used – one with a straight blade one inch wide, another with a curved, three-inch blade.

That, then, is the physical evidence from the remains – a large boat, shaped and hewn from solid timbers – but we still cannot say just how it would have looked when in use. What were the shapes at bow and stern? How high were the sides built up above the keel? E. V. Wright's own view is that it might have been rather like the Portuguese fishing boat, the *Meia lua*, in which the keel bends very sharply upwards and the side-strakes converge to a point. This would certainly have made the Ferriby boats seaworthy craft, yet they are ungainly creatures, making no real use of the flexibility of wood. Nevertheless, we have arrived at something which is a great deal more sophisticated than the simple hollow log. But how and when did this notion of building up the sides first appear? Sadly, we do not know, and the story is further complicated by the fact that although boats of the Ferriby type have not so far turned up again, the simple dug-out was still in use two thousand years later. When we come to the next major discovery in Britain, we have to leap forward many centuries.

Those intervening centuries are not entirely uncharted. We know a good deal about the vessels used by Britain's Roman invaders, though even they were not the first of our Mediterranean visitors. As long ago as 1000 BC the Phoenicians had come from Tyre to trade for Cornish tin. They had their own boat-building tradition, which we shall come back to later, but as it seems to have had little effect on native British boat-builders, for the moment we are going to stay with northern boats, which developed along quite independent lines. For a long time there were huge gaps in our knowledge of this area as well, but one at least was filled with the discovery of the Saxon burial ship at Sutton Hoo.

The vessel has been dated, so we know that it was buried around AD 625 and was probably built at some time towards the end of the sixth century. At the time of its discovery it was not the ship but its contents that attracted attention. It was a remarkable find. Here was the grave of a Saxon King, set to rest in a great ship with all his possessions around him – and what a treasure trove it was, of coins and jewellery, rich artefacts and everyday objects. Every aspect of life in Anglo-Saxon England seemed to be represented. After the excitement had died down work began on the ship itself. Unfortunately, however, much of the careful work done by the original excavators came to naught.

The Saxon burial mound at Sutton Hoo

The first part of the excavation was under the control of a local archaeologist, Basil Brown, who made the initial discovery when cutting into a burial mound; later Charles Phillips took over the work, and was joined by Lieutenant-Commander J.K.D. Hutchison of the Science Museum. The problem they faced was that of giving substance back to a ghost ship, for all the timber had dried out and disintegrated, leaving only an impression in the sand. It was precisely the reverse of the situation which Phillips was to face at North Ferriby, where the timber had been saved by that very mud which made work so difficult.

In this excavation, which took place in 1939, the entire ship was recorded in photographs and drawings. Although they were stored away at the outbreak of war, everything apart from the plans of the ship and the photographs was destroyed. It was decided that the whole site should be re-excavated in the 1960s, when the alarming discovery was made that not only the records but the site itself had suffered during the war. The army had been there, had dug a slit trench through the mound and trundled Bren-gun carriers over it, destroying much of the evidence that had existed in 1939. Nevertheless, a lot of useful work had been done, and the results that survived from the first excavation, together with the data from the new, enabled researchers to build up a quite detailed picture of the hull. As with the North Ferriby boats, the National Maritime Museum has mounted a display which gives a good idea of how this shadowy ship appeared.

This was a great open rowing boat 90 feet long by 14 feet beam, driven by 40 oars and steered by a single rudder or steering-oar that hung over the side to starboard. That, incidentally, is the origin of the word 'starboard'. In early boats it was common to have the rudder hung over the right-hand side of the vessel, looking towards the bows, which then became known as the 'steer-board' side. As it was normal to come into port with the opposite side of the vessel against the harbour wall so as not to damage the rudder, this side became the 'port' side. When we start to look at this ship in detail, we find some similarities to the Bronze Age boats, but rather more differences.

The similarities are superficial in one sense, yet important in another, for they suggest a possible direct line of development. As in the earlier boat, there is a keel-plank and the sides are built up from this, nine strakes to each side. This is where the similarities end. Instead of curving upwards, the keel is here extended vertically by means of separate stem- and stern-posts, while the side-planks overlap each other and are secured by metal rivets. Together, stem- and stern-posts, keel and strakes define the shape of the vessel, and the whole structure is then strengthened by 26 heavy wooden frames. This method of construction – building up the shell of the boat with overlapping planks and then strengthening that shell with internal frames – was the basic method used by northern shipbuilders right up to the fifteenth century. Known as clinker- or clench-building, it can still be seen in many small wooden craft today. Another feature which appeared in the excavation was the gunwale, extra planking added above the main body of the boat. On top of this were claw tholes for holding the oars, so that we do at least know that the boat was rowed.

The Sutton Hoo ship is so very different from the North Ferriby boats that it might seem slightly absurd to look for connections. Nevertheless, the same principles are at work. You start with a keel and build upwards and outwards, the planking giving shape to the boat. It is also conceivable, of course, that the techniques developed quite independently, and that other influences which are unknown to us might have proved decisive. In the absence of firm evidence, we are left with conjecture over likely lines of development. And that is not the end of the problems of interpreting Sutton Hoo. It is very tempting to assume that the vessel was typical of its time – but was it? Did those ancient Saxons choose from the very best ships of the day for a royal burial or did they, more prudently, select one that would not be missed? We can only surmise from the riches that surrounded the dead king that they provided the best. Did the boat have provisions for sails as well as oars? Again, we do not know. Sutton Hoo was a wonderful discovery, but it does not answer all the questions we want to ask about boat building in Saxon times.

At first sight the Sutton Hoo ship looks very similar to the more familiar Viking long ship. The latter, however, was in almost every way a superior vessel, with much finer lines. The native Britains learned much from the Norsemen, as the third of this trio of ancient boats testifies. These remains, which were found in marshland near Graveney in Kent, are those of a boat of the tenth century. Unfortunately, the remains are far from complete, and researchers have assumed that what they were confronted with was the stern extending for some 30 feet towards the midsection. The bow is missing, but what remains suggests that she was originally 45 feet long with a beam of about 9 feet.

Basically, this is another clinker-built boat, but because the actual wood remained and was recovered in 1970, it has been possible to establish a good many details about the construction. For a start, the stern-post itself leaves the keel at a very acute angle, overhanging the end by some 10 feet. This necessitates considerable curvature in the lower strakes – just what we see in contemporary illustrations of

The form of a great Saxon ship preserved in the sandy soil at Sutton Hoo

The Graveney boat, surprisingly well preserved but, unfortunately, incomplete. This is the stern section

medieval ships. The construction as a whole is far less crude than the Sutton Hoo one. Supporting frames are nowhere near as cumbersome and are joined to the strakes by wooden pegs, known as treenails. Constructional details are somewhat obscured by the fact that the ship appears to have been much patched in its years of service – and not all the repairers took as much trouble as the original builders, a phenomenon not entirely unknown today.

Particularly interesting is the evidence of the methods used to keep the boat watertight. Overlapping sections, such as the scarf between the keel and the stern-post, were kept dry by luting: that is, by putting hair between the two pieces of wood, the technique seen on the North Ferriby boats. The seams were caulked. Twisted hair was placed in the seams and rammed home by a caulking iron, an object like a cold chisel. The joints were then given further protection by a coat of tar – and here we have a technique which has lasted throughout the years of wooden sailing ships.

All three of these excavations are represented by reconstructions in the National Maritime Museum, and together they tell a story of increasing sophistication in hull design and hull-building techniques.

The clinker-built hull does, however, have its disadvantages. The overlapping planks produce an outer skin which is a long way from the smooth, streamlined ideal. Even more importantly, there is a limit to the size of ship that can be built in this way, working as it were from the outside in. The largest known clinker-built vessel was Henry V's *Grâce Dieu* of 1418, which had three layers of oak planking to provide the rigid shell. This shell was apparently built in its entirety before the internal framing was added. It was 200 feet long by 50 feet beam, and must have presented enormous problems to the builders. This technique was soon to give way to a new method – carvel building.

There are two basic ways to build: the one we have already seen, building a shell and then strengthening it, and secondly, building a skeleton and covering it. This latter technique was used in Britain in ancient times, for the small, portable coracles or the larger seagoing curraghs, with an animal skin as the outer covering. The distinguishing feature of the wooden carvel-built boat is that the covering planks abut to form a smooth shell. Much more significantly, the body of the ship is built up by laying down a keel, adding stem- and stern-posts, then filling in with intermediate frames which determine the whole shape of the vessel. The addition of planking for sides, floors and decks completes the basic structure. This is, of course, a gross

The clinker-built boat continued into the Renaissance. Though the exaggerated curvature of the hull might be artistic licence, the tools and the building techniques are accurate

over-simplification as shipbuilding was not and never has been quite that straightforward. Nevertheless, this form of skeleton construction, working from the inside outwards, rapidly became the norm for large ships, and remained so right to the very end. The carvel-built ship was to dominate shipbuilding from the end of the thirteenth century.

We shall be seeing many carvel-built vessels, but quite often size conceals the method rather than helping to explain it: the abundance of material, in the shape of floors and decks, can get in the way of a clear view of the whole structure. There is, however, a lovely example of a small carvel-built boat in the Windermere Steamboat Museum. It is an open yacht built in 1780, and looking at the hull one can see exactly how the frame has been put together to define the shape of a handsome, fine-lined craft. It is just 26 feet 5 inches long with a 5-feet 10-inch beam, built out of pine planking on an oak frame. That we can see it at all is due to the perseverance of Mr George Pattinson and his enthusiasm for all Windermere boats. He knew of the vessel, which had had an interesting career. It was built at Whitehaven and was owned by a local family from Belle Isle, Windermere, who kept it for 150 years. After that it seemed to vanish. Rumour had it that the boat had gone to Southport, where it was smartly pursued by George Pattinson, armed only with one faded photograph of the craft. He

The carvel-built boat: remains of an old ferry preserved at the Windermere Steamboat Museum

Carvel building on the large scale at David Williams' yard at Porthmadog. The frame is complete, ready for planking

found it upside down in a field, doing duty as a hen-house. The farmer agreed that modern corrugated iron would make a more effective cover than an eighteenth-century boat, so a bargain was struck. The iron went to Southport and the yacht came home to Windermere.

The best way to an understanding of wooden boat construction is to see it for yourself. This is no easy matter these days, but it is still possible to watch reconstruction work in which old methods and old tools are used, by visiting the Dolphin Yard Sailing Barge Museum at Sittingbourne, Kent. The Thames barge represents the most popular class of preserved working boats: where other classes are represented by single vessels, Thames barges come in dozens, most of them maintained by enthusiastic amateurs. As one barge-owner remarked: 'It's easy: you simply buy the boat, open up the hold and pour all your money inside.' Money alone does not guarantee a successful restoration – other requirements are skills and facilities, both of which the Dolphin Yard provides. It is very much a working museum, located in an old barge-maintenance yard on Milton Creek, an area which from the mid-nineteenth century was a major brick-making centre. Much of the huge output was carried in barges and one company, Smeed Dean, which in the years before the First World War was turning out 20,000 bricks a day, owned 61 sailing barges. These needed regular maintenance – hence Dolphin Yard.

The yard could tackle virtually any repair job, including ironwork, which was handled in the forge. The first approach to it if you come by land is a little surprising, disappointing even. There is no wide stretch of water, thick with boats and fluttering sails, as you would find at a new marina. Instead, a rutted track brings you through marshland to a narrow silted creek and a huddle of buildings. In the creek is a row of grassy bumps, representing the overgrown hulls of old barges, but at the yard itself there is almost invariably something going on, with owners and their friends constantly at work restoring old barges, often using the techniques of yesterday.

If one had to name one particular tool to act as a symbol for the shipbuilder's art, that tool would be the adze. It is an implement rather like an axe, except that the blade is not in line with the shaft but at right-angles to it. Its main function is to cut curves into a baulk of timber, and as the hull of a wooden ship is full of curved timbers, skill with the adze is a pre-requisite of any competent shipwright. In manufacturing the frames to which the planks will be attached to form the hull, the shipwright must aim for accuracy. In the clinker-built boat he could rely on a good eye – with carvel construction a little more is needed. The process is both longer and more complex.

A shipowner ordering a new vessel would naturally want to have some notion of what the finished vessel would look like, so a model had to be made. The model itself was often built out of interlocking sections, so that drawings could be taken from it and full-sized templates, or moulds, could be produced. It was from these templates that the actual wooden frame pieces were constructed. Accuracy at this stage was essential, for the frames determined the shape of the hull, and any misalignment in the frame would lead to distortion.

Curved timber is not only found in the frame: it is also to be seen in the planking of the hull. In the Bronze Age boat from Humberside,

23

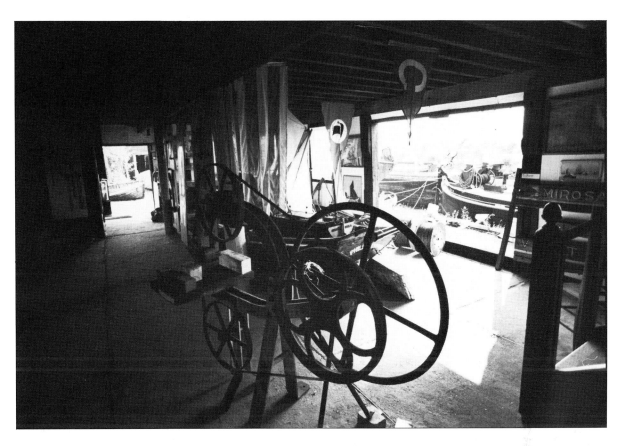

Old equipment is preserved – and used – at Dolphin Yard

strakes were of solid carved timber. The strakes of the more modern vessel are flexible planks, bent to shape. Traditionally, this was done in the steam-chest, and a steam-chest is still in use at Dolphin Yard. It is a simple enough device. Steam is produced in a boiler and then led off to a chest containing the planks. The wood responds to the damp heat and becomes pliable, so that after a suitable cooling period the planks can be easily bent on to the frame.

Conventional museums can advertise their wares in advance. Not the least of Dolphin's considerable attractions lies in the fact that activity is tied to the needs of the boat restorers who bring their barges to Milton Creek. One barge, for example, has been almost entirely restored at the yard, the aptly named *Revival*. She started life as the *Eldred Watkins*, when she was launched at Ipswich in 1901. She was in collision in 1934, when she sank, after which she was raised and given her new name. From 1938 she worked under sail in the explosives trade. Then in 1957, she suffered the indignity of derigging, her sails replaced by a diesel engine. Her working life ended in 1978 when the long task of restoring her to her former glory began. At the time of writing, that task is almost complete. Museum visitors have been able

Wooden barges in various states of repair and restoration at Dolphin Yard

Dead eyes and sheathes: just a few of the many items required in rigging out a vessel

Left. *A traditional job and traditional tools: Les George repairing a sail in the sail loft*

to watch the work in progress though there is never any guarantee as to what will be happening at any particular time. There may be a few tidy-minded individuals who like to know what to expect when they pay a visit; others will enjoy the fascination of ever-changing activity. Certainly visitors will come away with a unique insight into the techniques used in building wooden boats.

The journey from the simple, hollow hull of the ancient boats to the carefully-designed hull of the Thames barge, specifically aimed at a special job of work, is a long one. But the complexities multiply when we begin to look at the methods man has devised to move that hull through the water.

2   *Setting Sail*

Sailing is an ancient art, and an apparently straightforward one. Hold a sail up to the wind and the wind will blow you along. Most children will have made matchbox boats with paper sails and sent them scudding across the murky waters of the bathtub. The child has the advantage over the real-life sailor: he has only to move his head for the wind to change direction. The sailor, alas, has to make do with what he gets.

In designing a practical sailing boat many factors have to be taken into account, two of the most important of which are how to make the maximum use of what wind there is, and how to make progress regardless of which way the wind happens to be blowing. Sailing is not limited to going forwards with the wind coming from behind the boat, because the sail does not act like the paper version in the child's bathtub boat. The wind blowing across the face of a sail has, one could say, a double action. Since the sail itself is soft and pliable, it curves as the wind flows over it, and when the airflow is smooth, there are two forces at work – a 'pulling' action on the front of the sail and a 'pushing' action behind. This has been known to generations of seamen, but it is only recently that we have come up with a term to define the phenomenon – the sail acts as a 'flexible aerofoil'. Coining a definition does not help us to sail a boat nor even to design a better sail, but it does help towards an understanding of how the sail works.

The earliest sailing boats for which we have any very positive information as far as Britain is concerned are those of the Viking raiders, traders and settlers. Although these were primarily rowing boats, with as many as 30 pairs of oars, the long ships were also fitted with a single mast, on which a square sail suspended from a horizontal yard could be hoisted. The yard ran across at right-angles to the fore and aft line of the vessel. This is what we call a square rig, and this same general pattern was to remain in use for several centuries. The single-masted, square-rigged vessel was used for trade and war, in rivers and estuaries and on the longest voyages. Over those centuries there were, of course, many changes. Cargo vessels developed, with much more rounded hulls and deeper keels, and the Viking ships' woollen sails, which stretched and sagged, were replaced by canvas. Just as importantly, steering methods were changed. The steering-oar hung over the side of the vessel gave way to the familiar rudder hinged on the stern-post. The hull itself was often more elaborate than in the earlier vessels, being built up at both ends with superstructures known as forecastle (fo'c'sle) and aftercastle. Nevertheless, the main features remained the same in British merchant ships. They were clinker-built, rounded hulls with a square sail on a single mast. This basic pattern was retained in one type of vessel which can still be seen under sail – the Humber keel.

The Humber Keel and Sloop Preservation Society's vessel, *Comrade*, would not be out of place in a medieval painting. At first it might seem something of an anachronism – like the coelacanth, it is an

The hundred-year-old fishing lugger, Barnabas

unlikely marine survivor which should, by rights, be extinct. The world has come a long way since medieval times, so why has progress left the keel behind? The short answer is that it has not. Ship development, particularly in the design of sailing ships, is not a continuous smooth movement from a crude beginning to a single desirable end. Vessels vary because the jobs they are required to do vary, and the Humber keel is a splendid example of a vessel that was ideally suited to a particular set of circumstances.

Comrade is what is known as a Sheffield boat, which is to say that she could travel as far inland as the Yorkshire city of steel, and had to be able to cope with the shallow waters of canal and river as well as with the rough, deep waters of the estuary and even the journey out along the east coast. These were special requirements that imposed special conditions on the boat builders, and the first thing they had to cope with was size. To reach Sheffield the keel had to pass through locks, and there would be no point in building a vessel larger than the smallest lock it would encounter. Look up Bradshaw's *Canals and Navigable Rivers of England and Wales* and you will find the following information on the largest vessel that could navigate as far as Sheffield:

Length	61'	6"
Width	15'	6"
Draught	6'	0"
Headroom	10'	0"

The simple, square-rigged ship, with forecastle and aftercastle. St Nicholas Rebuking the Tempest *by Bicci di Lorenzo*

Humber keels at the beginning of the century

These are the dimensions of the Sheffield boat, built with bluff bows, straight sides and a rounded stern, to fit snugly into the locks and to provide a hull which contained the maximum amount of cargo space. In fact, the hull is almost entirely usable cargo space allowing the keel to load up to 100 tons. Low bridges account for the low headroom, but as 10 feet would be impossibly low for a mast, some method had to be devised for lowering it at bridges. The mast had to be tall, because the keel often moved through tree-lined waters and through towns where buildings came to the water's edge, so a large sail that stood high above the obstacles was essential in order to catch whatever wind there was. If, however, you have to carry a lot of sail on a tall mast, and that mast has to be frequently raised and lowered, then you must keep your rigging as simple as possible – and the square rig is as simple as any and simpler than most. The more we look at the keel, the more we understand how well she was suited to the particular circumstances of her working life. But to understand fully just how well she fitted her task, you have to see her on the water under sail.

Comrade has her berth in the appropriate setting of the busy old port of Hull, where she is surrounded by her close relations, the barges that still ply the river – but now with the benefit of engine rather than sail. She is easily distinguished from the rest by her tall mast, set slightly forward of midships. Built in 1923, she shows one important difference from her predecessors: she is constructed with an iron rather than a wooden, clinker-built hull, but in all other ways she is identical, and her sailing characteristics remain the same. No one

Right. Barnabas under way in a stiff breeze off Falmouth

Preparing to hoist sail on the keel Comrade

would describe the keel as a sleek vessel, those bluff bows and almost flat stern giving her something of the shape of a date-box. She looks what she is, a working boat. Nevertheless, she is handsomely fitted out, with a carved rail round the stern.

The keels were always well kept, as they were often home to the skipper and his family. The main cabin lies under the decking of the stern, and is as comfortable as such a small space allows. Beds are tucked away into large cupboards and a stove provides welcoming warmth after a day spent in the all too prevalent cold easterlies of this coast. In many cases, the family helped crew the boat, and were especially useful during canal travel when, if there was an adverse wind, the boat had to be hauled through the water. In the days before power tugs – or when costs had to be kept low – this meant hiring a horse and a 'horse marine' to manage it, or the whole family getting out on the towpath to pull the vessel along by hand.

The major part of the deck space is taken up by tarpaulin-covered hatches over the hold, and although that hold utilises the major part of

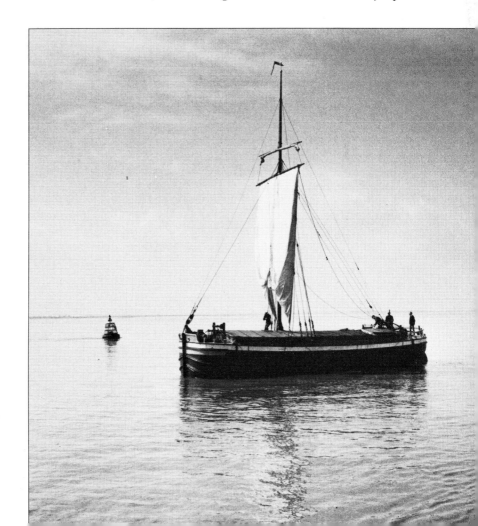

the hull, the load is still comparatively small, not profitable enough to support a large crew. The working crew consisted of no more than two men or, often as not, a man and a boy. To help them, they had an array of winches around the deck, and as the vessel prepares to make sail, it becomes very clear why they are needed. With such a small crew, and with heavy equipment to handle, mechanical assistance is essential. The mast, which pivots in a box on the deck known as a tabernacle, is raised and lowered by means of a hand-operated winch or roller. The keel has two sails, a mainsail and a smaller topsail above it, each of which is suspended from a horizontal timber, the yard. These are raised up the mast by halyards – an abbreviation of 'haul yards' – and these, too, are worked by winches. Having got the sails up, they still have to be set in the right position, in relation to the direction of the wind and the direction in which the vessel is supposed to be travelling. This is where the seamanship of the skipper comes to the fore.

It is a common belief that such simple square-rigged vessels can only sail with the wind more or less astern. This is a complete fallacy, and perhaps the most remarkable discovery to be made by anyone fortunate enough to sail on *Comrade* is just how close to the wind she can sail. The yards and sails are manipulated through the running rigging, as opposed to the standing rigging which is used to steady and support the masts and spars. There are two main components to the running rigging – sheets and tacks. When the vessel is being sailed towards the wind, the sail has to be kept quite flat – that is to say, instead of running at right-angles to the fore and aft line, it is brought in more or less along that line. The foremost lower corner of the sail is attached to the tack which pulls that part of the sail towards the bow; the aft corner is pulled towards the stern by the sheet. Now the vessel is underway, sailing at an angle to the wind. The same sail setting can be left untouched, with the skipper easing or tightening the sheets to make fine adjustments for as long as the vessel continues to travel in the required direction.

If the wind is coming from astern, it might be possible to hold the course for long periods. If it is not, then the vessel can only make progress by following a zig-zag course – that is, the vessel must tack. And that means that the whole mainsail has to be moved round. The tack is slackened on one side, and pulled taut on the other, and similarly, one sheet is slackened and the other tightened. So if the sail started off running from starboard and forward to port and aft, it would be reset so as to run from port and forward to starboard and aft. It is one of those functions which sounds complex when described but which suddenly becomes simple when seen in practice. As the line of the sail changes, so the direction of the boat can be changed too.

Even under an efficient crew, changing tack takes a finite amount of time, and during that time there is a mid-point when the sail simply hangs slack and the vessel virtually comes to a halt. The amount of

All sails set, but becalmed

*Left. Comrade making good
speed with the wind in her sails*

*Fred Schofield, sailing master
of Comrade*

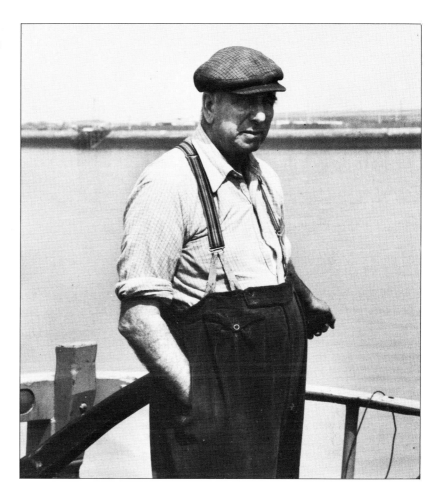

time needed for the operation depends in large part on crew efficiency,
and *Comrade* is fortunate in having a superbly skilled skipper in their
sailing master, Fred Schofield. His crew may be enthusiastic amateurs,
but he has been a keel-man all his life. He appears to know every inch
of the Humber estuary, demanding a course alteration to clear a
sandbar totally invisible to the rest of us. He knows every inch of
Comrade, too, for she was his ship in her working days. Yet even under
his expert control, that moment must come when the sails are ren-
dered useless while they are being reset. If they could be swung across
almost automatically, by the action of the wind as the tiller was put
over, then the problem would be removed. This would be possible if
the sails were, in some way, hinged at the mast – a system which can be
seen at work in the Society's other vessel, *Amy Howson*.

The hull of *Amy Howson* is virtually identical to that of *Comrade*, but
her rig is entirely different. In the square rig, the wind always blows on
the same side of the sail – if it catches the reverse, then the sail, and the

ship with it, are blown back. This alarming and potentially dangerous action is known as being taken aback, a term which like so many other nautical expressions has found its way into everyday speech. With the fore and aft rig of *Amy Howson*, things are very different. If the wind catches the opposite side of the sail, the sail can be blown to the opposite side of the vessel which, properly handled, can set straight off on the opposite tack. The fore and aft rig, then, has certain advantages, but there are many variations on this overall pattern, and at least one crucial intermediate step.

Left. *Hoisting the foresail on Barnabas*

Right. Barnabas *sails off in a good breeze, with the Cornish flag flying*

A feature of fore and aft rig is that the actual sail is asymmetrical, most, if not all of the sail lying behind the mast. This has certain advantages in terms of sailing characteristics, but the same effect could be obtained using a square rig with an asymmetrical sail, which instead of being suspended from its mid-point would be suspended closer to the narrowest side of the sail. This would be a very efficient sail, with excellent qualities in terms of sailing close to the wind. It would, however, suffer from one disadvantage. In the keel, when you change tack, you swing the sail round and it takes up the same basic configuration while

simply pointing in a different direction. If you tried to do the same thing with the asymmetrical sail, you would end up with the major part of the sail forward of the mast instead of behind it – quite the opposite of what was intended. To keep the correct configuration, you would have to dip the yard from which the sail was hung and move the whole thing bodily round the mast. And that is precisely what happens with vessels carrying a dipping lugsail.

Barnabas is a wooden fishing boat, built a century ago as a mackerel driver in St Ives, Cornwall. She has been preserved by the Maritime Trust and is now regularly sailed from her home port of Falmouth. Although only 36 feet long, she has two masts – a main, or more accurately a foremast, in the bows, and a mizzen in the stern, thus leaving the midships quite clear for the principal business of fishing. Working the little boat is not easy. At the end of a tack, the heavy yard of the mainsail has to be lowered and carried round the mast, the sail has to be bundled up and carried round the mast too, while controlling hands cope with the running rigging as in the keel. During the whole operation, the helmsman has to keep control of the tiller. What is more, when wind conditions change during sailing, there is yet another process to be added to keep the crew busy. In *Comrade*, the sail area can be adjusted by reefing. Reef-points are short lines attached to the sail, which are tied up to shorten it. In the lugger, sail is shortened by removing the large sail and its yard and replacing it with a shorter yard and smaller sail.

It might seem that the dipping lugsail has been specially designed to make work. The largest keels, up to 70 feet long, can be managed by a crew of two – *Barnabas*, at half that size, requires a crew of five. It appears nonsensical. Yet when you sail in *Barnabas* her special qualities soon appear. She sails remarkably close to the wind and in a stiff breeze she heels over, at which point she reveals that she is a match for any of the fibre-glass and alloy specials that sail out of Falmouth. There is, it must be admitted, an inclination to feel very smug as one's century-old wooden fishing boat outpaces a modern yacht. Speed in such a boat matters, for the working fisherman always wanted to be first to the fishing grounds to get the best position. Manœuvrability is also important: the fisherman had not only to reach the shoal but to stay with it. Even so, is it not ludicrously wasteful to carry those extra crew just to achieve that little bit of extra speed? It might be so if they did nothing else; but all those hands were absolutely necessary for handling the nets. So what may superficially appear to be wasted manpower turns out in practice to be a sensible method of making the best possible use of a large crew.

The lugger is a boat well adapted to a particular job – just how well adapted will be clearer when we look at fishing in more detail in Chapter Five. This theme of 'horses for courses', or ships designed to fit specific circumstances, recurs throughout maritime history. A

Lowering the sail: the main yard is being lowered, while an energetic crewman leaps to gather in the sail

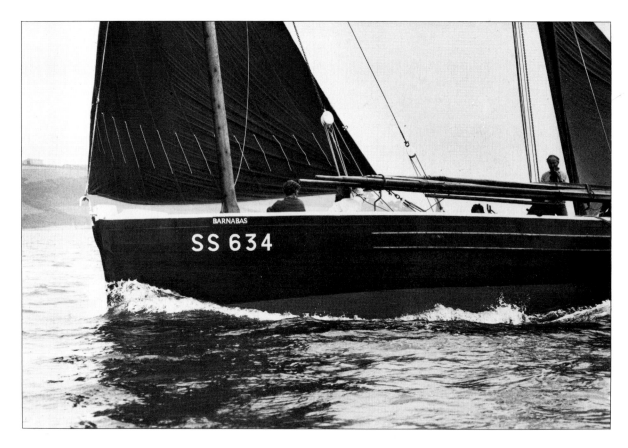

splendid example is the Norfolk wherry. Like the Humber keel, it is a cargo vessel trading mainly on inland waters, with occasional forays around the coast. The waters in this case are the rivers and lakes of the Norfolk Broads. Here handiness and manœuvrability are prime virtues and, as with all such cargo vessels, the smaller the crew the greater the profit. The wherry is another two-man boat, but the rig is now a complete fore and aft.

Albion, built in 1898, and the one surviving working wherry still afloat, is preserved by the Norfolk Wherry Trust. She is 48 feet long by 15 feet beam with a mere 4-feet 6-inch draught, and is built on altogether finer lines than the Humber keel. A comparatively small vessel with a registered tonnage of only 23 tons, she manages to carry a single sail with the great area of 1,400 square feet. Although this might seem excessive for a small boat, it has to be remembered that in inland waterways, the wind does not blow as freely as it does on the open sea. Traditionally, the wherries were clinker-built, with 14 oak strakes to each side though, as with other vessels, iron and steel eventually took over from wood. There were only two massive beams in the frame, leaving a large hold covered by hatches. The narrow side-deck was seldom more than a single plank width, and when fully loaded the decks were right down to the waterline.

The 40-feet-high mast is set well forward, and as with the keel it can be raised and lowered. Here, however, it passes below the deck, where there is a counterweight of over a ton. The mast has to be

Barnabas *showing a good turn of speed, despite her hundred years*

Right. *The wherry* Albion *built in 1898, in her working days, at Bungay Staithe*

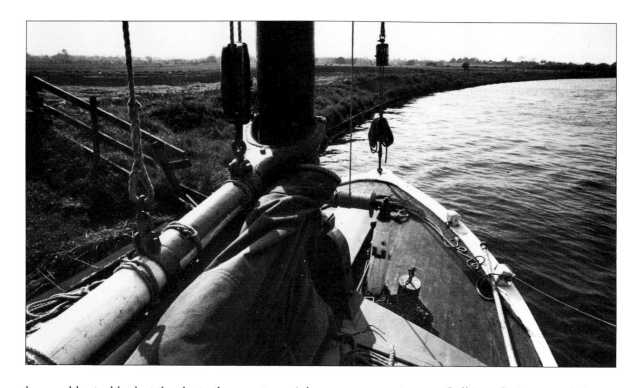

lowered by tackle, but thanks to the counterweight comes up again as if by magic when released. The sail is hung from a yard, one end of which is shaped as a jaw to fit round the mast, so that the yard itself runs back towards the stern. This is known as a gaff rig, and although it was to become quite common, the wherry retains its own, unique features. The long, heavy spar with its great spread of sail would appear to be scarcely manageable by a two-man crew, but the difficulties are minimised, while the gear is kept simple. A single halyard and winch are used, but the actual yard, the gaff, is controlled through two blocks. The one nearest the mast, the crutch block, rises until it can go no further and the luff, the edge of the sail next to the mast, is quite taut. Then the second block comes into play, raising the peak, the far corner of the sail. So, with one man on the winch and another controlling the gaff line which stops the gaff swinging around, the whole operation is completed with the minimum of fuss. The sail is up and the wherry is ready to go.

Albion herself is regularly sailed by charter parties, under the direction of her skipper Ewan Anderson. Sailing out of Thurne with a stiff breeze well abaft the beam, *Albion* shows her paces, slicing through the water with a fine turn of speed. The great sail is managed by the skipper from his position at the tiller, through the sheets which come ready to hand. A careful watch is kept on the sail itself and on the masthead vane, which stream out in the wind. These vanes, a full

Gaff jaws fitting around the mast of Albion

Raising sail on Albion, the throat of the gaff is rising up the mast

With the throat of the gaff in position, the peak begins to rise controlled by the gaff line

fathom long, are a feature of wherries, and they are attached to spindles which carry ornate metal silhouettes. Sailing with the wind, is, as usual, something of a luxury to be enjoyed when available. If the wind direction does not change, then the river direction does. Round a sharp bend goes the boat, the pennant swings at the masthead and now the boat must tack in the unfavourable wind.

The sheets are controlled through sheet-blocks which slide along an iron bar, known as the 'horse', set athwart the vessel. On any particular tack the block will be right over at one end of the horse, the sail stretched out over the water on that side of the boat, and the wherry will be heading more or less towards the bank. To make progress along the river, the boat will have to tack. In the narrow confines of the river, the quicker this can be achieved the better, and the long period of adjustment needed to alter a square rig would be most inconvenient. Here the gaff rig comes into its own. The wind can be taken on either side of the sail, so at the end of one tack, as the tiller is put over, the sail shakes loosely for a moment before the wind catches the other side. Then it fills with wind, swings across over the hatches and the block shoots along to the opposite end of the horse. The wherry is off on its new course.

Albion *sailing well in a good breeze*

Even the versatile gaff rig cannot cope with all weather conditions – and no sailing vessel can sail without a wind. When the wind resolutely refuses to blow, the wherry-man has no option but to move the boat himself, and this involves 'quanting'. The quant is, in effect, an overgrown punt-pole. Starting at the bow of the boat, the wherry-man throws the pole at an angle into the water, leans his shoulder on the butt and walks down the side-deck towards the stern. Reaching the stern, he pulls out the quant and marches down to the bows to start all over again. It is not such hard work as it might seem – at first. The boat moves easily enough through the water, but after a while even the most enthusiastic quanter can be heard whistling for a wind.

Albion remains virtually as she was in her trading days. True, there are now bunks in the hold instead of cargo, but if those were lifted out she could go back to work tomorrow. There is still a well-appointed captain's cabin in the stern – and there is still no engine. Those who go out on *Albion* have only two options if they want to get anywhere – sail or quant. In this respect, she is very different from that other class of river and coastal sailer, the Thames barge, whose auxiliary motors are mere standbys. The barges are preserved and cherished for their fine abilities under sail.

A misty, still morning and the quanters are hard at work

It is perhaps a little misleading to talk of 'the' Thames barge, for Thames barges come in a wide variety of shapes and sizes, with many variations in rigging. The sailing barge has its origins in the dumb barges and lighters, craft which moved with the tides and currents of the Thames, crudely-steered vessels that were used to load and unload the big seagoing vessels that rode at anchor in midstream. At their simplest these barges were little more than open boxes, which were first improved by giving them rather more gracious lines. Bow and stern were built with a pronounced slope, rather as in the modern punt. These overhanging ends were known as 'swims', and from such beginnings a whole class of barges developed known as 'swimmies'. Add a simple square sail on a short mast and you have the first recognisable Thames sailing barge, though its sailing capabilities were, to say the least, limited. By the end of the seventeenth century, it became common to see a new type of rig on British waters and on the Thames in particular. The innovation arrived from Holland, one of the great maritime nations which did as much as any other to advance boat design. The new vessels still carried a square sail, but it was set fore and aft, with the peak extended by a sprit, a spar which ran from the foot of the mast to the far, upper corner of the sail. The rig came to be known as the spritsail rig, and once it had been introduced on to the Thames barge in the eighteenth century, it became the distinguishing feature of that vessel.

The spritsail was not new when it came into use on the Thames barge, but even in its more primitive forms it had many of the charac-

Raising the mast after shooting Acle bridge

Above right. *Preparing to set sail on* Comrade *on a calm day in the Humber*

Right. PS Waverley *leaving Dunoon pier*

A Thames hay barge off Sheerness around 1900

Left. SS Great Britain: the construction using overlapping, riveted plates is very clear

teristics that were to make it so suitable for this type of vessel. As in the wherry, the clew, the lower aft corner of the sail, is controlled through sheets, while the upper end of the sprit is controlled through two separate ropes, the vangs. The bottom of the sprit rests in a rope collar, known by the curious name of 'snotter', which in turn is held in place on the mast by a rope running down from the masthead, the standing lift. One great virtue, in a boat that has to be worked by a small crew, is that the spritsail itself can so easily be handled. The sail is furled by brailing, that is, pulling it in to the sprit and the mast, in much the same way as the old-fashioned theatre curtain was pulled back and up.

We are fortunate in having details of a Thames spritsail barge of the eighteenth century, for one was described in Chapman's *Architectura Navalis* of 1786. Her hull was essentially that of the swimmie, but she carried a spritsail and a triangular jibsail forward of the mast. She also had one other feature, which was to remain an essential of the sailing barge – a pair of lee-boards. Seagoing vessels normally have pronounced keels which prevent them slipping sideways in the water in a beam wind. The barges which needed to ply shallow rivers had no such keel, but the lee-boards were able to do the same job. They are heavy wooden boards, either pear-shaped or triangular, which are suspended at the side of the vessel, ready to be lowered into the water when needed. Like the spritsail, the lee-boards were introduced from Holland. It was an important innovation, for fitted with lee-boards the barge was no longer just a river boat, but became a seaworthy craft that could take her place in the coastal trade.

Development continued over the years, and the spritsail barge ended up very different from the old box on the water. The hull was given finer lines, and sail area was increased. A topsail was added above the mainsail, and vessels carried as many as three jibs. A short mizzen mast was added at the stern, with the boom attached to the rudder. The diminutive sail did little to help drive the boat forwards, but it did a great deal to assist manœuvrability in narrow waters. This was further improved by the replacement of the tiller by the wheel. As ships grew larger, it became more and more difficult to manage the tiller. Some help was provided by devices such as the whipstaff, which was basically an additional lever between tiller and rudder to ease the work. The steering-wheel attached to the rudder through a system of ropes or chains was a great advantage for large craft. And Thames barges became really quite large in comparison with either Humber keels or Norfolk wherries.

Typical of the many restored spritsail barges is *Anglia*. She was built in 1898 in Ipswich and worked in the grain-carrying trade, entirely under sail, right through to 1960. She had an uneventful working life, though she was at one time in the ownership of a colourful

The spritsail barge Anglia *at Dolphin Yard*

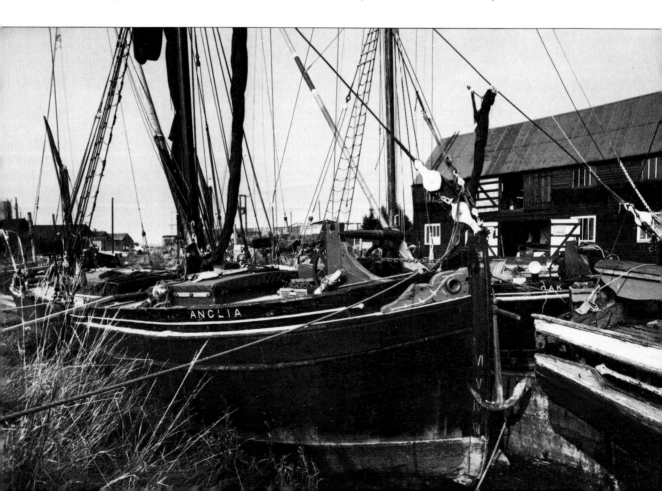

character known as Gentleman George Ventris, so called because of his ability to charm a cargo out of any potential customer. It might seem surprising that she continued under sail for such a long time, but the Thames barge withstood the competition from motor vessels, not to mention the ubiquitous motor lorry, longer than any other North European sailing craft. That it did so was thanks to its efficiency, much of which is due to those barge matches begun in 1863 by Henry Dodd. There is no longer the same pressing need to improve sailing efficiency, but the matches are no less fiercely contested now than they were a century ago.

While sailing in *Anglia* in the 1981 Medway match, that efficiency was amply demonstrated. The rigging of a barge of this size, 83 feet 6 inches long by 20 feet 6 inches beam, is much more complex than that of the simple gaff-rigged wherry. There is a small mizzen set far back in the stern, and a topsail can be set above the mainsail, while an extra staysail can be added above the foresail – and when it comes to racing, everything is set. Although the boat behaves in a similar way to the gaff rig, there is rather more work on board for everyone to do. The main sheet runs across a horse as in the wherry, but there is an extra horse for the foresail sheets. In coming about, if you want to make the best possible turn, everything has to be done at just the right time. Mainsail swings across first, followed by the foresail, while one lee-board is raised and the one on the other side lowered. In its working days, the barge may have been managed by a crew of two, but not on race days.

Anglia belongs to the staysail class of barge. Bigger vessels do take part in the race: these are the bowsprit class and they require even more handling. As the name suggests, a sprit is extended out from the bows, allowing large foresails to be set. In the Medway match these big boats set off half an hour after *Anglia*, but caught up and passed her long before the finishing line was reached. Henry Dodd would have been delighted to see the efficient sailing barge still racing over a century after he started the first event.

It is tempting to see the move from simple square rig to complete fore and aft as a progression in design. This is not the case at all. All the vessels we have looked at have survived through to the present precisely because their particular characteristics suited them to the task they were called on to perform. Though there is no single one that can be described as intrinsically better than the others, each represents years of improvement on the first basic design. The square rig of the Humber keel is a long way from the rig of early Viking and Saxon boats. The improvements themselves came slowly, for shipbuilders are notoriously conservative creatures. Just occasionally in its long history, shipbuilding has taken a sudden leap forward into a new age. In Europe, that happened with the appearance of the fully-rigged ship in the fifteenth century.

3   Sail and Steam

The vessels we have looked at so far have all been comparatively small, mostly single-masted. Throughout the medieval period and on into the 1400s, there was a steady if unspectacular improvement in hull and rigging design, but the norm for merchant ships remained the clinker-built hull, square-rigged on one or two masts. Change began to accelerate in the fifteenth century, when northern shipbuilders began taking tentative peeps over their own back walls to see what their neighbours to the south were doing. Ideas that had once been limited to particular regions began to spread. Mediterranean vessels had long been driven by the lateen sail, a triangular sail suspended from a long yard which hung at an angle to the mast. They had also long used carvel instead of clinker construction. Both these ideas now began to be incorporated into northern boats.

The most famous ships of the fourteenth and fifteenth centuries were the carracks of Spain and the caravels of Portugal. The carracks were originally two-masted ships, with a large square sail on the mainmast and a much smaller mizzen set close to the stern. During the fifteenth century, these ships increased dramatically in size, rising from a maximum of around 250 tons at the beginning of the century to 1,000 tons at the end of it. Such large ships could not possibly be worked with the traditional two masts and simple sails. The three-masted ship had arrived.

The caravel was the more important of the two types. Like the carrack, it developed as a carvel hull with three masts, but was given lateen sails on all three masts. The lateen works rather like a dipping lug. It has the same excellent characteristics in sailing to windward, but at every change of tack the huge spars had to be lowered and carried round the mast. The Portuguese compromised, building the caravel redonda, a vessel that combined ingredients from both northern and southern traditions. It was a mixture of square and lateen rig, the most popular version being square-rigged on fore and main masts, lateen rigged on the mizzen. It was in such ships that the great voyages of discovery were made. Caravels took Columbus to the New World.

From the fifteenth century onwards there were to be further great changes in sailing-ship design, but none so dramatic as those which transformed local traders into great ships of exploration. The lines of development had, in fact, now been set. From now on, all big wooden vessels would be carvel-built, with three or even more masts and with any combination of square and fore and aft rig that seemed suitable for the job in hand. The unwieldy lateen was soon to disappear, giving way to the more manageable gaffsail or spritsail, but there was no fundamental new principle at work.

As early as the seventeenth century, the Dutch had begun experimenting with two-masted ships, fore and aft rigged on both masts, which they called schooners. The name was kept for all multi-masted fore- and aft-rigged vessels. The schooner was to become very popu-

Steam gauges on the paddle steamer Waverley

57

lar, particularly in North America. It could be built to quite a large size, but only required a comparatively small crew, since all the sails could be handled from the deck with the aid of machinery. Crew size was an important factor in reducing expenses, and finding large crews could, in any case, be quite a problem in a young country with a small population.

Schooners also found favour in Britain, particularly in circumstances that called for small but fast ships. For the exotic fruit trade, for example – oranges and lemons from the Azores, pineapples from the West Indies – speed was essential, as there were no buyers for holds full of rotting fruit. By the middle of the nineteenth century, there were well over 200 schooners employed in the trade, supplying London with some 60 million oranges and 15 million lemons a year. Another equally profitable trade was found in carrying fish from Newfoundland. But the trade which kept the schooner going into the middle of the twentieth century was rather less romantic. The coastal schooners, scurrying busily around the British coast and across to Ireland, carried such mundane cargoes as coal and pit props. Where once there were hundreds of these craft, now there is just one lone survivor, the *Kathleen and May*.

The schooner Kathleen and May, *with her topsails removed*

Kathleen and May was launched in April 1900 at Connah's Quay, Clwyd (then Flintshire), but on that day she was named *Lizzie May* after the owner's two daughters. She received her new name in 1908 when she was sold to an Irish owner, equally proud of his own two daughters. So *Kathleen and May* she became, though the other two young ladies were never quite forgotten, for the new owner kept the old ship's bell with the original name. Her later career plots the decline of the schooner trade. At first she had a busy life. Her cargo book for June 1900 shows her leaving Rochester for Plymouth on the 2nd with 220 tons of cement. On the 22nd she was on her way to Cardiff from Plymouth with 225 tons of pitch. On 1 July she moved on again to Falmouth with 210 tons of coal and from there she took 225 tons of china clay to Weston Point before finally making her way back to Rochester, travelling light. In her first eight years, she covered nearly 40,000 miles and carried nearly 25,000 tons of cargo.

Under her new owners, there was less variety in the cargo. Coal was at the heart of their trade, and *Kathleen and May* plied back and forth across the Irish Sea, carrying coal from the Forest of Dean through the Severn port of Lydney or Lancashire coal through Garstang. It was largely a one-way traffic, and in time the trade began to look gloomy. In 1931 she was sold to Captain Jewell of the famous schooner port of Appledore in Devon, but it was a sad day for the ship. Her masts and sail were reduced and an engine installed. Her days as a sailing ship were all but over. She continued to trade, though with decreasing success, right through to 1960. A happy ending seemed unlikely, but fortunately she was purchased by the Maritime Trust in 1970. The long job of restoration began, and *Kathleen and May* is now one of the finest vessels in the Trust's collection of historic ships, berthed in St Katharine's Dock in London.

If one was to ask what typified the West Country schooner of which *Kathleen and May* is an example, then the obvious answer would be a description of the main features: three masts, fore and aft rigged on all three, but with a square-rigged topsail on the foremast, an arrangement that gave them their other name – topsail schooners. One could also provide another answer, for they had one other characteristic in common: variety. No two schooners were ever quite alike. Individual owners would approach a shipbuilder with a list of requirements – size, type of cargo to be carried, preferred rig and so on. The builder then produced a half-model of the hull, which was all that was necessary, the vessel being symmetrical. Plans were rarely drawn, since the owner would probably not have understood them.

Once the model was approved, it was sliced up into sections. These sections were taken to the mould loft, where they were scaled up to full-size drawings from which the frames could be constructed. Success or failure of a design owed less to the rule-book than to the individual designer's eye and feel for shape. Now the keel could be

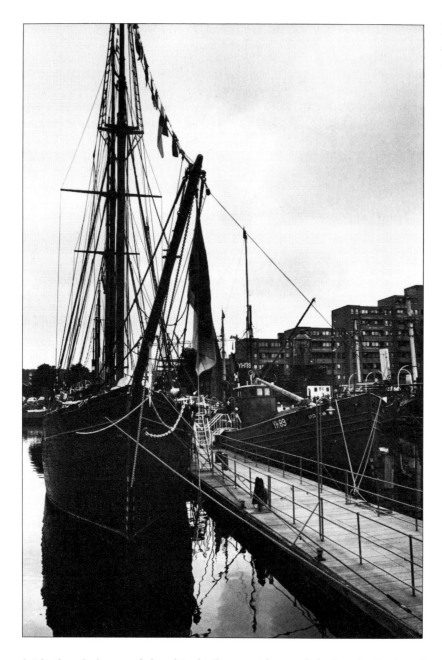

Kathleen and May *in her permanent berth in St Katharine's Dock, London*

laid, the skeleton of the ship built up, sides and decks planked and caulked: another schooner was ready for launching. Masts and rigging were added later in a fitting-out berth.

Kathleen and May emerged from this process as a wooden vessel, 98 feet 5 inches long, 23 feet 2 inches beam and 10 feet draught, with a cargo-carrying capacity of 226 tons. She had three masts, each built out

The deck area, with mizzen mast and boom

of two sections, the main one rising 78 feet above the deck. With all sails set, she carried 4,550 square feet of canvas. She had the usual schooner rig, with both upper and lower square topsails and a triangular foresail and three jibsails attached to the bowsprit.

The crew to handle this expanse of canvas was comparatively small. There were four hands housed in the fo'c'sle, and the captain and his mate had their cabins in the stern. The captain was able to keep an eye on progress even when he was below decks, for there was a compass mounted in the ceiling above his table. This small crew worked hard for their livelihood, as indeed did their ship – before she found her last berth after more than half a century at sea.

Vessels like *Kathleen and May* played an important role in the local trade, but the schooner suffered from one major disadvantage. You cannot go on increasing the size of a fore and aft sail without eventually making it totally unmanageable. An alternative is to increase the number of masts, and in 1902 the Americans launched the unique seven-masted schooner, *Thomas W. Lawson*. She remained a curiosity and even she was never intended for more than the coastal trade. When really big ships were needed for long voyages, the designers turned back to the square-rigger, and of these the most prestigious were the fast tea, wool and grain clippers.

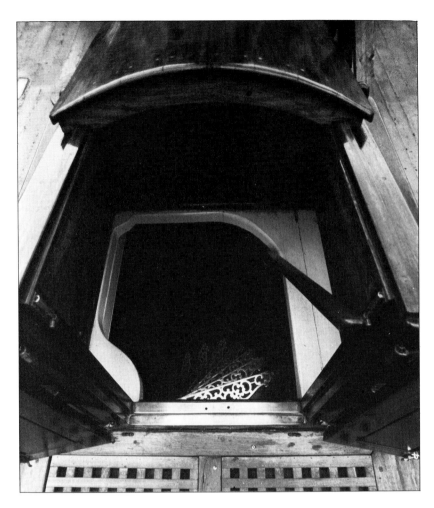

Left. *Ornate spiral companion way leading down to the saloon*

Below. *The saloon, used by captain and mate*

The Cutty Sark in her trading days

It is tempting to think of the clippers as the ultimate development of sail – and so they were if speed is your criterion. Yet there were other craft which could take far greater loads. If there is not, and never can be, the 'ultimate' sailing craft, it is nonetheless true to say that few vessels have had more appeal to the world at large than the clippers. It is our great good fortune that we have, in Britain, one of the most famous of them all: the *Cutty Sark*.

The clipper, like the schooner, was developed in America. The New World was the great centre for new ideas in the world of shipping. The British merchantman at the beginning of the nineteenth century was big, sturdy – but slow. The Americans began the hunt for speed during the war of 1812, when they began building privateers. After the war, cargo vessels began participating in two illicit and unsavoury trades, opium- and slave-trafficking, in both of which speed was of the essence. The cargo vessels were not able to take huge cargoes, but they could escape capture. Thus it came about that the clippers, perhaps the most beautiful ships ever to sail the oceans of the world, had their origins in war, drugs and slavery. They continued, however, and developed to·carry on more attractive trades.

In 1832, a vessel was built at Baltimore, the *Ann McKim*, which had all the characteristics of the clipper. She was square-rigged on three masts. She was long and shapely, with a length-to-beam ratio of 5 to 1, and she had that most distinctive of all clipper features – steeply-raked, hollow bows. She created a sensation in America, and soon even the conservative Europeans had to take notice. The new, fast ship and her successors soon began to monopolise a lucrative trade: tea from China. A premium was paid for the first loads of tea to reach London each year, and the Americans were taking the prize. The British had no option but to join the race, and try their hand at clipper construction. The American lead was eventually lost, not to superior British design, but because the country collapsed into Civil War. American clipper building stopped, and the British established a lead they were never again to lose. The race was now exclusively between British ships.

In 1868, *Thermopylae* was built specifically to win the China tea race, and in 1869 *Cutty Sark* was commissioned to challenge her. They were both too late, for in that same year, 1869, the Suez Canal was opened and the tea trade passed from the clipper to the steamer, the latter having been vastly improved by the introduction of the compound engine (see p. 89). There was still, however, another trade left for the clippers: the wool trade from Australia. In 1883, the *Cutty Sark* began her new career as a wool clipper, and two years later she acquired in Captain Richard Woodget the master who was to make her undisputed champion of the trade. For ten years, from 1885 to 1895, she made the fastest runs, achieving her best performance in her final year under Woodget, when she completed the journey from Sidney in 67 days. In 1895, she was no longer showing a profit and was sold off to

Left. The Cutty Sark, *the nearer of the large vessels at the quay, loading up with wool at Sydney*

Right. The Cutty Sark *today*

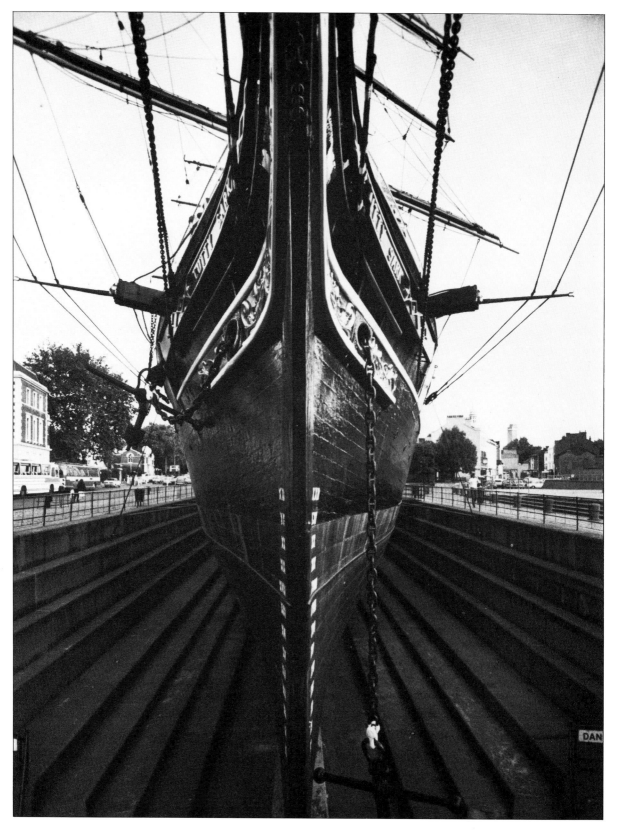

66

spend the next 27 years sailing under the Portuguese flag. In 1922, she was blown into Falmouth and was spotted by Captain Wilfred Downman, who bought her for £3,750. By the time the deal was completed, *Cutty Sark* was back in Lisbon, but she was towed home for restoration and installation in her last dignified home at Royal Greenwich.

Seen today in dry dock, the first, overwhelming impression is of the sheer beauty of her lines. Even those with no experience of ships and ship design can tell at a glance that she was built for speed. The lower part of the hull is sheathed in a copper–zinc alloy as protection against the *teredo navalis*, the mollusc known as the ship's worm, which bored its way through many an old wooden ship. To see the actual construction of this ship, you need to go inside. There, instead of planking on a wooden frame, we find that the outer shell is attached to an iron framework. This development, using the new techniques of the industrial revolution, will be looked at more closely in Chapter Six. For the moment, it is worth looking at some other features of the hull construction. Only the very best materials were used. Rock-elm was used for the lower strakes, varying from 11 to 6 inches in thickness. Side-planking and the upper deck are in teak, the lower deck in pine.

With her very fine lines, the *Cutty Sark* has nothing like the cargo space of the slower bulk carriers, so every inch of hull space had to be used to the full. During her days in the wool trade, the bales were pressed in with screw-jacks, until the entire hold was almost one solid mass of wool. On her last run, they managed to cram in 5,000 bales. There was no space here for the crew. They had their home in deck-houses and a crowded fo'c'sle, and very cramped it must have seemed in the months spent continuously at sea. Originally, there was only one deck-house for a crew of 28. A second was added later, and the complement was reduced to 24: Captain, First and Second Mate, boatswain, carpenter, sailmaker, 8 apprentices, 8 seamen, cook and steward. Later still the numbers were reduced to 19. This seems an amazingly small number when you come up on deck and look at the masts and spars.

From the top of the mainmast to the deck is just 8 inches short of 150 feet, and around the 3 masts one can see the complex of yards and rigging that held and controlled the great area of canvas that was spread when all the sails were set. And what a spread that was, a total of 34 sails, 32,000 square feet of canvas – three-quarters of an acre. It is hard not to feel sad when looking up at spars from which sails will never again hang or be filled with wind. But we are looking on in comfort: there is no need for us to turn out on a black night of gales off Cape Horn, to climb those tall masts, to work out along the yards to fight with stiff, wet canvas. The clippers were ships of great beauty, but they represented danger and hard work to the men who sailed them.

There is one strange feature on this ship – the figurehead. The lady who graces the bows is conventional enough, but she holds a clump of

The sleek hull and sharp bows of the clipper

hair in one hand, and to know why you have to know how the ship got its name. She was built in the Clyde, by the partnership of Hercules Linton, designer, and William Dundas Scott, engineer, and where else should one go for the name of a Scots-built ship than to the work of Robert Burns. The owners settled on the tale of Tam O'Shanter, who was almost bewitched by the sight of a beautiful girl dressed only in a short shift or cutty sark. The girl was indeed a witch, and as witches cannot cross water, Tam galloped across a bridge, leaving the witch in her cutty sark, holding the hair from his horse's tail.

The main mast

Everything in its place: all rigging lines had to be kept in good order and ready at hand

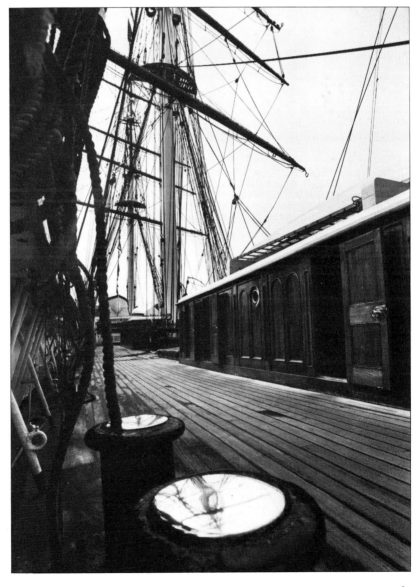

Deck-houses for the crew

The *Cutty Sark* is the last survivor of a great class of merchant sailing ships, yet she was built almost a full century after the first steam-engine appeared on the water. It is a common belief that the arrival of the steam-engine spelled the death of sail, yet apart from the archaeological discoveries we looked at early on, every vessel we have seen was built in the age of steam. How did it come about that the two could co-exist for so long? To answer that question we have to understand the limitations of steam at sea and the problems faced by engineers and designers.

The steam-engine was one of the great inventions of the industrial revolution. It first appeared as a pumping engine, with a piston rod at one end of a large rocking beam and pump-rods at the other. It was soon appreciated, however, that by replacing the pump-rods with a sweep-arm and crank you could produce a rotary engine. Such engines soon took their place alongside the old water-wheels as prime movers for the new industries. It requires very little imagination to see that those two sources of power could be joined together and put to work. In the water-wheel, the movement of the water turns the wheel, and through the shaft it can then turn whatever machine you attach to the shaft. Reverse the process, however, and use a steam-engine to turn a shaft, and you can turn the water-wheel and use it to move water. Set the whole lot on a floating platform and you have a paddle-steamer. Just such a system, with a beam-engine attached to a paddle-wheel, came into use in some of the most famous of all paddle-steamers, the stern-wheelers of the Mississippi. The story of the paddle-steamer does not start there, however, nor even in Britain, the home of the steam-engine, but in France.

J. C. Périer was the first to build a steamboat, which he tried out on the Seine in 1775, but the cylinder was too small, the pressure too low, and his experiment failed. Eight years later, after a few unsuccessful ventures, the Marquis Claude de Jouffroy d'Abbans built the 182-ton paddle-steamer *Pyroscaphe*, which puffed its way up the River Saône near Lyons. Other experiments followed apace. In America, John Fitch tried various forms of paddle-boat, including one in which the engine worked a series of oars, and James Rumsey built a boat that was way ahead of its time. Water was pumped in at the bows and pushed out at the stern, producing a form of jet propulsion. His craft carried out a series of successful trials on the Potomac in 1787 and on the Thames in 1793. No one was interested.

In Britain, experimentation began when Patrick Miller tried out various types of paddle-boat, powered by a gang of men – the principal result of which was the total collapse of the crew. He turned perforce to steam, and his design was executed by William Symington in 1788 and given its first trial run on Dalswinton Lake in Scotland. The event was noteworthy for having Robert Burns on board, making him possibly the first poet in history to have been moved by steam. As a result of this

The paddle-steamer Comet,
built in 1812

trial run Symington was asked to build a second boat for commercial trials on the Forth and Clyde Canal. The boat, the *Charlotte Dundas*, was a success, but the canal proprietors feared damage to the banks and declined to take the matter further. The chain was not, however, broken, for the tests were watched by the famous American engineer, Robert Fulton, who went on to build his own steamboat, the *Clermont*. She went into operation on the Hudson in 1807: the world's first successful commercial steam service had begun.

In 1812, Britain too got a commercial steamer, the *Comet*, built by John Robertson of Glasgow for Henry Bell, a hotel proprietor from Helensburgh. She went into service on the Clyde, operating between Glasgow and Greenock. She then did service in the Firth of Forth and, after modification, worked up and down the west coast until she foundered on Craignish Point in 1820.

Comet's original engine was preserved and can be viewed in the Science Museum in London. Its links with the earlier beam-engines are clear to see, and it bears a resemblance also to early locomotive engines of the pre-Rocket era, whose ancestry she shared. The main features are the single 12½-inch-diameter cylinder set over the crankshaft and driving through side rods on to a pair of side levers, so that it is rather like an upside down beam engine. The crankshaft has a six-foot diameter flywheel and a pinion, the latter providing the connection to

Left. Comet's *engine,
preserved at The Science
Museum, London*

Right. *The last sea-going
paddle-steamer* Waverley

turn the shafts and their paddles. It is, taken as a whole, somewhat
crude and inefficient, but it did begin the long story of paddle-steamers
on the Clyde, a saga which continues to the present day.

Glasgow is the great manufacturing city of Scotland, and in the
nineteenth century that meant it was also dirty, overcrowded and
unhealthy. But the city has the great advantage of standing on the
River Clyde which, once clear of the city, boasts some of the most
beautiful scenery in Britain. The paddle-steamers offered the link
between the two – taking day-trippers round the Firth or delivering
them to the popular resorts of Dunoon and Rothesay. The heyday of
the paddle-steamer came at the end of the nineteenth century when a
whole fleet of resplendent vessels plied the Clyde, offering food,
drink, scenery and – without exception – music. This could be anything from the 'Berliner Philarmonisches Blas-Orchester', which
played on a special cruise in 1901 on the *Duchess of York*, to less
highbrow musicians as described in the *Glasgow Herald* of 1888: 'A

penny brass whistle and a cracked violin. . . . Go where one would,
the maddening sounds followed. In desperation, I gave the musicians
a shilling to play among a crowd of Sunday-school children in the
forecastle.' Today, there is just one paddle-steamer left on the Clyde,
the *Waverley*, and she has the added distinction of being the last
seagoing paddle-steamer at work anywhere in the world.

    Waverley was built on the Clyde by A. and J. Inglis in 1947. She was
by no means the first to bear that name. Her immediate predecessor,
Waverley III, was built in 1899 and was sunk in 1940, when she was one
of the many vessels that steamed across the Channel to take part in the
evacuation from Dunkirk. The fourth *Waverley* was built for the London and North-Eastern Railway and that too puts her in a great
tradition, for the old North British Railway had begun running paddle-
steamers as early as 1865. *Waverley* is 235 feet long and 30 feet beam,
and in her trials she sped through the water at a very respectable 18.5
knots. Her working speed is normally about 14 knots: paddle-steamers
had come a long way since *Comet*.

For many passengers the chief delight of a trip on *Waverley* is not the music (that, too, is a tradition that continues), nor the scenery, nor even the bars, which stay open throughout a cruise, but the engine. Every passenger is able to see it at work, for instead of being shut away in a closed engine-room, the machinery is out in the open in the centre of the ship, with walkways around it. This has been a feature of Clyde steamers since the beginning of this century, when Captain James Williamson of the Caledonian Company decided that paying passengers might find the sight of the great steam monster interesting. They did, and they still do.

The engine is not only far larger and more powerful than that of *Comet*; it is also more complex, having three cylinders. It is, in fact, a triple-expansion engine, but that is a development we shall be looking at in the next chapter. For the moment, we shall just be noting the change in scale. Whereas the cylinder of *Comet* was a mere 12½ inches in diameter, the smallest of *Waverley*'s is 24 inches, the next 39 and the largest a huge 62 inches, the three working together developing 2,100-indicated horsepower. Whereas *Comet*'s cylinder was vertical, as in the old beam-engines, *Waverley*'s are horizontal, providing a direct drive without the use of side-levers. Other differences between the two vessels are less immediately apparent. The early paddle-wheels were simple rigid blades set on an axle; in the modern steamer the blades are jointed so that they can feather, reducing their resistance through the water after they have finished work.

Left. *The shapely paddle-boxes*

Right. *Musical entertainment on board* Waverley

The tiny eagle provides the clue that Waverley's engine was built at the Eagle Foundry

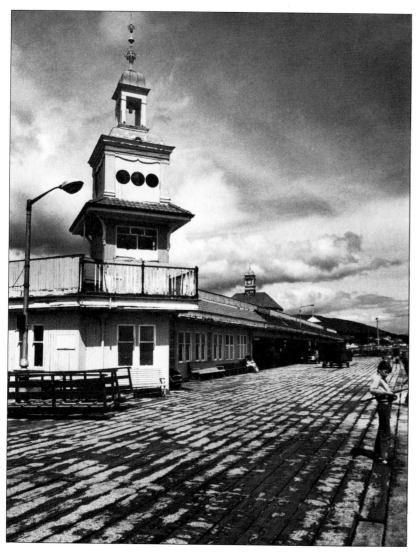

The steamer signalling system on Dunoon pier. The circles indicated which steamer had priority for moorings

The great versatility and manœuvrability of the paddle-steamer can be seen when she has to turn, at such spots as Helensburgh on her Clyde trips. Using forward and reverse, she can turn if not on the proverbial sixpence, in a space not very much larger, though this manœuvre is not permitted on British passenger vessels. This is one of the attractions for owners of paddle-steamers – though all enthusiasts for the craft will also point to the character and beauty of the vessels, and *Waverley*, with her twin funnels, attractive lines and shapely paddle-boxes, is as fine an example as any.

Long before *Waverley* took to the water, engineers were looking for alternatives to the paddles as a means of propulsion. The paddle-wheel is not the only device that can be used for shifting water, and the Archimedean screw, if less widely used, is of almost equal antiquity. It was to the screw, then, that engineers turned their attention. There were a number of unsuccessful trials with screw propulsion in the eighteenth century, but it was not until 1836 that two engineers patented screw-propellers: Francis Pettit Smith and John Ericsson. The latter's version had two drums, each fitted with seven blades, and there were successful trials in 1837. There was not, however, any great enthusiasm for Ericsson's ideas, and he took himself and his invention to America, where we shall meet him later.

Smith was more immediately successful. He started life as a farmer, and his first experiments were with clockwork models on the duck pond. Originally he used a screw with two full turns. When this was accidentally broken in half, the screw's performance, much to Smith's astonishment, increased dramatically. This led to larger-scale experiments, first with a launch, the *Francis Smith*, then with a bigger vessel, the aptly-named *Archimedes*. She was launched in 1838, successfully circumnavigated Britain and later made a journey to Portugal. The screw-propeller had successfully proved its worth. There was, however, one argument still to be settled. Which was the more efficient – paddle or screw? This was settled in a most dramatic fashion in 1845, when two identical frigates were fastened together stern to stern. *Rattler* was screw-propelled, *Alecto* had paddles. The order 'Full Ahead' was given, and *Alecto*, her paddles thrashing the water, was towed backwards at nearly 3 knots.

One vessel of much the same size and with much the same sized engine as the pioneering *Francis Smith* has survived. The latter was 32 feet long, 5½ feet beam and had a 6-inch-diameter cylinder to her engine. Over on Lake Windermere is *Dolly*, 41 feet long, 6½ feet beam and with a 7-inch cylinder engine. And even the dates are not very far apart, for *Dolly* was built around 1850.

Lake Windermere has been home to a rich variety of steamboats for well over a century, and of these quite the most magnificent are the privately-owned steam launches. A selection of these lovely vessels is now preserved at the Windermere Steamboat Museum: preserved not as dead exhibits, static behind glass cases, but as working boats, still able to make their elegant way over the waters of the lake. *Dolly* is the *grande dame* of the collection. Her life was comparatively staid until 21 February 1895. On that day, a young woman was lying in bed, waiting for her baby to appear, and from her window, she could see *Dolly* out on Ullswater. Next time she looked, the boat had gone: *Dolly* had sunk.

Dolly remained on the floor of the lake for over 60 years until a local sub-aqua club came across her, almost lost among the weeds. In 1962, she was successfully raised and taken back to Windermere, where she had begun her days. Slowly, the pine and oak of her hull were dried out and the time arrived for the testing of her engine. The fresh water of the lake had none of the corrosive effects of salt water, and the metal appeared to be sound. So it proved. *Dolly* responded as if she were just out for another trip after a weekend off, and she is still regularly steamed today. The only alterations to her original machinery are those that have had to be made to meet modern safety requirements. Elsewhere the old still serves – *Dolly* even has her original piston rings!

Durability is not the least of the appeals of old boats and old machinery. We live in an age of almost instant obsolescence, so that to find a machine such as *Dolly*, well over a century old, sunk during the freeze-up of 1895 and still running, seems a minor miracle. It is not just

Tug of War between the screw-propeller of Rattler *on the left and the paddles of* Alecto *on the right*

Dolly, *the nearer of the three vessels, in the boat shed at Windermere*

Dolly's *simple, single cylinder steam engine*

Dolly's *original boiler*

that *Dolly* can claim to be one of the world's oldest mechanically-powered boats, but that she has achieved that distinction in spite of having spent 64 years submerged. She is a vessel which amply demonstrates the virtues of simplicity. The boiler is simple: just a single, return flue. The engine is simple, put together by a local blacksmith and pushing the craft through the water at a very modest 5 knots, a speed quite comparable to that of the pioneering *Francis Smith*.

Simplicity is the keynote, also, of her visual appeal. Her elegance has nothing to do with elaborate fittings, and everything to do with the sweet curves of her hull. She was to have some much finer successors, which we shall look at in the next chapter, but the Windermere Museum would be worth a visit even if *Dolly* was the only vessel on view. Just seven years before *Dolly* took to the water however, another screw-propelled steamer was launched, just about the most revolutionary vessel every built – the *SS Great Britain*.

Full Steam Ahead

At a meeting of the directors of the newly established Great Western Railway in 1836, one member expressed dismay at the idea of a railway line as long as the one proposed, which was to join London to Bristol. The Company's engineer scoffed at the doubters and declared that for his part he saw no reason why the line should stop at Bristol. Why not build a steamboat, call it the *Great Western* and carry on to New York?

The engineer was one of the world's great inventive geniuses, Isambard Kingdom Brunel, and his notion was by no means impractical. An American ship, the *Savannah*, had already used steam on a transatlantic crossing in 1819, but the engine was only regarded as an auxiliary and the paddles were actually lifted out of the water when not in use. The engine was, in fact, only in use for 85 out of the 659 hours that the crossing took. Brunel's plans were for something quite different – he wanted a big ship, with large, powerful engines that would be in use throughout the entire crossing.

There were many who argued that such a ship was an impossibility, because it would have to carry so much coal that there would be no room left for passengers or cargo. Large engines would be more efficient than small, but it was generally held that increase in size would not solve the problem, because doubling the size of the ship would mean that twice as much power would be needed to move it through the water. It was Brunel who demonstrated the essential flaw in this argument. Resistance to water depends on the area of hull in contact with the water, a dimension expressed in square measure: carrying capacity depends on the volume of the hull, a cubic measure. You do not increase the power needed to move a vessel in the same proportion as you increase its size. On 28 July 1836, work began on the *Great Western*.

A rival company, the British and American Steam Navigation Company, was thinking along similar lines. When it became obvious that their ship would not be ready in time to challenge Brunel's new vessel, they hastily altered the small steamer *Sirius*, originally intended for nothing more ambitious than trips across the Irish Sea, and sent her off on her pioneering journey from Cork to New York in April 1839. The great question still had to be answered: could the steamer carry enough coal for the voyage?

Sirius's owners took no chances: every inch of the holds was packed with coal and there were piles of it on the deck. Even then she very nearly ran out of fuel. Stories circulated at the time that she had only completed the trip by burning furniture, doors and even one of her masts. They were not true, but she was down to her last 15 tons. The *Great Western*, twice the size of *Sirius*, began her voyage 4 days after *Sirius* and very nearly caught her up, arriving only a few hours later, having taken 15 days 5 hours against *Sirius*'s 18 days 10 hours. Brunel's enthusiasm had been vindicated: the case for the big ship had been made.

The steam launch Swallow *on Lake Windermere*

By now, Brunel was already working on an even bigger vessel, the *Great Britain*. In this one ship, first announced as the *City of New York*, Brunel brought together virtually all the important elements that were to characterise the ocean-going steamer for the next hundred years and more. The new ideas did not appear all at once. In the original scheme, she was very similar to the *Great Western*, which was 236 feet overall by 35 feet beam (60 feet if you include the paddle-boxes) and 16½ feet draught. It was decided quite early on that she should be faster than her predecessor, which involved a bigger engine and a slightly larger hull. In January 1839, the even more radical proposal was made not to build a wooden boat at all, but to construct the hull of iron, with riveted wrought-iron plates fastened on an iron frame.

The concept of the iron boat was not new: John Wilkinson, the ironmaster from Coalbrookdale, had built an iron barge which was launched on the Severn as early as 1787. Extra impetus had been given to the use of iron by the introduction of Cort's puddling process, which had ensured good, cheap supplies of wrought iron. For just as iron has greater strength, bulk for bulk, than wood, so wrought iron is stronger than cast iron. But if the idea of an all-iron hull was not new, the notion of an iron hull of these dimensions most certainly was. And throughout the planning stage the ship kept growing, so fast that she acquired a new name to match her size: *Mammoth*. As finally built, she was 322 feet overall, 51 feet beam and 18 feet draught, with a gross registered tonnage of 3,720 tons.

The design of the hull alone would have ensured the new ship a place in history. The wrought-iron plates, 6 feet by 2 feet 6 inches, were overlapped, as with the planks of a clinker-built boat, giving her hull great strength. She was also very safe, for the hull was divided into watertight compartments. The shape was very different from that of the *Great Western*. Whereas the first vessel had had straight sides, the sides of the new ship had a pronounced curve, and she was graced by a clipper bow, a demonstration that Brunel was not in the least averse to borrowing good ideas from other sources. The innovations did not stop there.

1838 was the year for experiments with screw propulsion, and in 1840 Smith's *Archimedes* visited Bristol. Brunel was at once intrigued, and although work on an engine to turn paddle-wheels was already well advanced, he decided to change to screw propulsion. The unhappy man who had designed the original engines, Francis Humphreys, saw all his work scrapped, and the strain and disappointment literally killed him. But work on the new engines and the propeller went ahead.

The engine had four cylinders, each 88 inches in diameter with a 72-inch stroke, inclined upwards towards the crankshaft at an angle of 66°. Between the two crankpins was an 18-feet-diameter drum, round which were wrapped chains to take the drive down to a smaller wheel

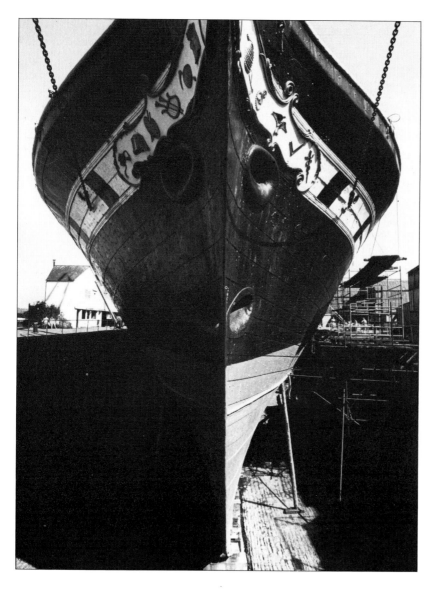

Clipper bows with ornate decoration: seen from this angle, the Great Britain *has much in common with the* Cutty Sark

on the propeller shaft. The propeller itself, designed by Brunel, had 6 blades 15 feet 6 inches in diameter, the largest ever built at that time. Steam was provided by a double-ended boiler at the comparatively low pressure of 15 pounds per square inch (p.s.i.). However, she was not dependent on steam alone. She carried sail on 6 masts, and habitually used sail and steam together.

A special dry dock was built at Bristol for the construction of the great ship – and a handsome sight she must have appeared, as she gradually took shape. She was as beautiful inside as out, with large state rooms, cabins and promenade decks. She not only represented a revolution in marine engineering, she also offered a whole new concept in passenger comfort.

On 19 July 1843, Prince Albert travelled on Brunel's Great Western Railway to christen Brunel's new ship with her final name, *Great Britain*. The dry dock was flooded and the ship carefully eased out of

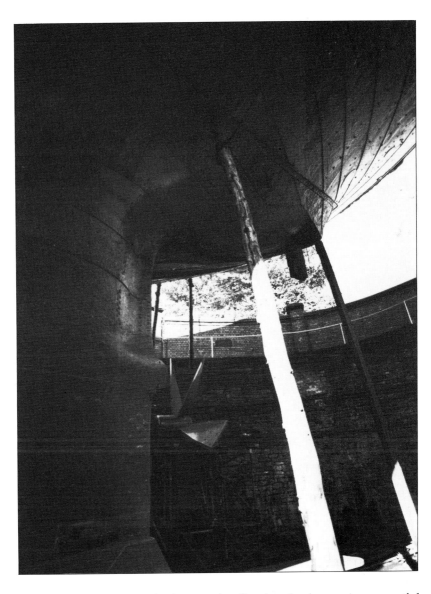

Stern and replica propeller

her very tight-fitting dock into the floating harbour. A successful maiden voyage was begun on 23 January 1845, which proved more of a test than was intended, for she met tremendous seas off Lundy, and was hit by a wave estimated as 60 feet high. In July of that year, she made her first voyage to New York, completing the crossing with 600 tons of cargo and 50 passengers in just under 15 days.

Her later career was, to say the least, not without incident. In September 1846, she ran aground on the east coast of Ireland, and there she lay right through the winter. The long and expensive work of salvage finished off her owners. *Great Britain* was sold, and passed through many hands before eventually ending up as a coal and wool hulk in the Falklands. There she was beached and abandoned: it seemed that she was destined to end her days there. But Brunel's iron ship was not to be so easily destroyed, and though abandoned she did not break up. In the 1960s, plans were laid to bring her home.

For those who love ships there can have been few more moving sights than that of Brunel's ship coming home to Bristol under the great span of Brunel's bridge across the Clifton Gorge. Today she is back in her original dock, where the slow work of restoration continues. There is still a long way to go before the work is complete, but her present state does at least provide ample opportunity to study her construction, for with her fittings long gone the great hull lies open, the skeleton exposed. What one cannot see is the engine, and it is engine design that has changed most dramatically since Brunel's day.

Left. *The upper decking of* Great Britain, *recently restored*

Right. *The Clyde puffer* VIC 32, *tied up at her moorings in Tarbert harbour*

The *Great Britain* showed that the future lay with big, iron ships, steam-engines and screw propulsion. Yet her engines were far from perfect. Steam pressure was low and fuel consumption high. It was the problem of fuelling the steamers that did more than anything else to keep the great fleets of sailing ships at work. The solution to the problem was obvious, if not simple to achieve: improve the efficiency of the engines. Just as the early massive steam-engines owed their basic design to the mine-engines of the eighteenth century, so now the way forward was shown by two Cornish mine-engine designers, Jonathan Hornblower and Arthur Woolf.

The easiest way to increase the pressure of a steam-engine would appear to be to increase the pressure of the steam. To do so first involves increasing the efficiency of the boilers; and just such an increase occurred in the decade from 1850 to 1860. However, this only works up to a certain point, beyond which the steam goes into the cylinder, pushes at the piston, and finally passes out of the exhaust, but still under pressure. The solution found by Hornblower and Woolf was compounding. Instead of letting the high-pressure steam simply blow away, they led it to a second cylinder to work again: they built engines with small high-pressure cylinders which were coupled to bigger low-pressure cylinders. Such engines found a multitude of uses, for example in ships, the first marine compound engine being fitted to the *SS Brandon* on the Clyde in 1854.

VIC 32 steaming through the Kyles of Bute

Over the years many vessels were fitted with compound engines, and one class has earned a special place in the affections of all lovers of steamboats: the Clyde Puffers. These sturdy little craft served as general cargo carriers up and down the west coast of Scotland. They carried anything and everything, and being flat-bottomed could go almost anywhere and even be beached. They got their name because in the original form, when steam was exhausted from the second cylinder, it was sent up the funnel in a series of puffs. The design changed around 1925, with a fundamental modification to the low-pressure cylinder. Instead of puffing out into space, the exhaust steam was condensed in a separate condenser. This created a vacuum below the piston, which one could think of as a kind of negative pressure, increasing the efficiency of the engine. The condensed steam also ensured a supply of fresh water for the boilers, which otherwise would have been fed with salt water, with great loss of efficiency. This design was used in the Second World War for the VIC Puffers, the Victualling Inshore Coasters, which provisioned the fleet. One of this class, *VIC 32*, has survived to steam on along the traditional Puffer routes among the sea lochs and islands of the Scottish west coast.

At first sight, *VIC 32* is every child's bathtub boat grown up, a chubby little vessel, with derrick at the front, wheel-house and funnel

The wheel house of VIC 32, *complete with the captain's tomato plant*

at the stern. She appears every inch a working cargo boat, but appearances in this case are deceptive. The exceptionally well-informed Puffer enthusiast will spot that the hatch coamings have been raised by nearly 2 feet, and going below into what used to be the hold one soon sees why. Whereas once there would have been a large single cargo space, there is now an intermediate deck, dividing the space in two. The upper deck now holds saloon and galley, while the lower has cabins.

VIC 32 is still a working boat, but now she pays her way by carrying passengers: holidaymakers with a taste for Scottish steam. Each weekend through the summer season, she lies at her berth among the fishing boats in Tarbert harbour, simmering gently and ready to go. Her trade may have changed but her character has remained the same, and this, for those of us who have holidayed on her, is her greatest charm. None of this would come as any surprise to the most famous of Puffer skippers, Neil Munro's splendid character Para Handy, who remarked of his own broken-down tub, the *Vital Spark*: 'She was chust sublime! She should be carrying nothing but gentry for passengers.'

The real enthusiasts inevitably head first for the engine-room. The boiler is of a cylindrical, vertical type, producing steam at 120 p.s.i. for an engine with a high-pressure cylinder $10\frac{1}{2}$ inches in diameter and a low pressure of 22 inches. To get the necessary work out of *Great Britain*'s engines, supplied with steam at a mere 15 p.s.i., Brunel had to use 4 cylinders, each of 88 inches in diameter, which is perhaps an indication of how far engine design had come since the 1830s. The engine is not just a compound, but also something of a hybrid, since each cylinder has quite different mechanisms. The high pressure is fitted with piston-type valves, while the low has D-type slide-valves. The links and eccentrics are in line with the crankshaft. A number of pumps are also worked by steam: a feed-ram to keep the boiler supplied with water, air-pump, bilge-pump and a condenser circulating pump, feeding salt water into the condenser.

For those who are only accustomed to the throb and vibration of the modern diesel, there is the delightful discovery to be made that steam is smooth and almost silent, the only noise being the steady slurp of the condenser-pump and the occasional blast on the steam whistle. Holidaymakers are given every opportunity to discover the delights of steam travel, being invited, but not forced, to try their hands at stoking. In the heat of the boiler they discover that there is another side to the romance of steam: hot, hard work. They may also discover something of the pride of the engineer who keeps his brasses clean and the 50-odd lubrication points oiled every hour.

Another feature of *VIC 32* is her old working machinery, still in first-class condition. The steam-winch is regularly used to lift a dinghy into and out of the water, just as in her working days the same winch was used for cargo. Externally, she is almost the same as she has always been, and the changes which have been made have done nothing to affect the essentials of one of the last coal-fired steamers.

Compounding did not end with the addition of a second low-pressure cylinder. Improved boiler design made it possible to produce steam at even higher pressures. The use of the condenser meant that here was a ready supply of fresh water, instead of the sea water which deposited salt in the boilers. Multi-tubular boilers, of the type introduced on to the railways by George and Robert Stephenson in 1829, were brought into ships, and eventually the Scotch boiler with a cylindrical shell and internal fire-tubes came into almost universal use.

The advance in boiler design may seem less exciting than the development of engines, but was just as important. The higher pressures that became available meant that simple compounding was inadequate if pressure was not to be wasted and in 1871, Benjamin Normand patented the triple-expansion engine in France. Now the marine engine could be said to have reached its true working efficiency, and the way was beginning to open to competition with sail on all the sea routes of the world. Greater fuel efficiency meant greater profits, and also necessitated fewer calls at the complex chain of coaling stations.

The triple-expansion engine is, as the name suggests, an extension of the two-cylinder engine by the addition of a third cylinder between the high-pressure and low-pressure cylinders. In large vessels, these engines became so large that it is often impossible to see them all at

The steam-powered steam launch Otto

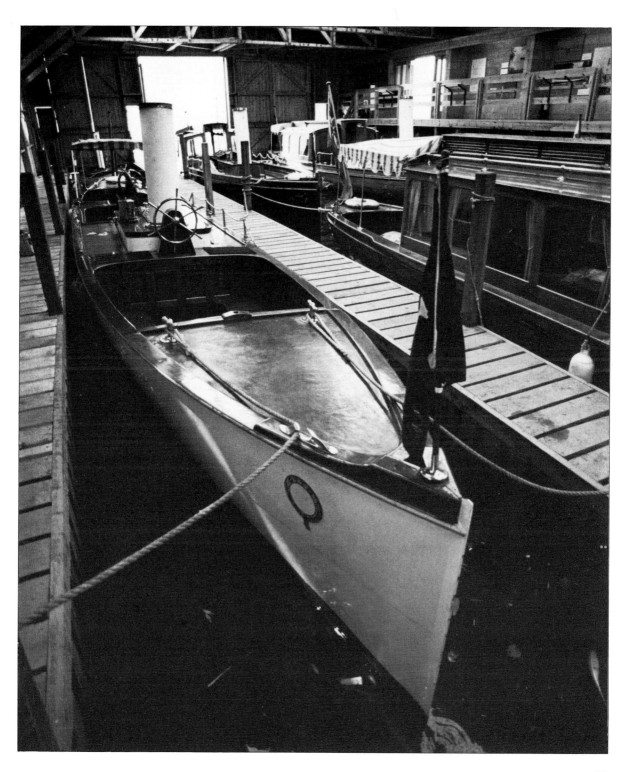

once, for they can spread upwards over the space of two decks. One can, however, see exactly what a triple-expansion engine looks like and see it at work when it is scaled down to fit a steam launch. There is just such a launch in the Windermere collection: *Otto* floats alongside *Dolly*, and the contrast is immediately apparent.

Windermere boats can be roughly divided into two categories: those built primarily for comfort and those built primarily for speed. *Otto* comes in the latter group. Built in 1896, she has the sleek steel hull of the racer. She has a functional rather than a decorative elegance, and her engine is very much the centre-piece of the whole craft. Steam is provided by a locomotive-type boiler at a pressure of around 200 p.s.i., from where it is led to cylinders of $6\frac{1}{4}$, $8\frac{1}{4}$ and $10\frac{3}{4}$ inches in diameter. The steadily increasing size of the cylinders compensates for the steadily decreasing pressure of the steam. This particular array could produce a speed of around 16 knots. *Otto* is also interesting in that the hull was initially bolted together rather than riveted, having been sent to Windermere in sections from the makers at Wivenhoe, Essex. There she was re-erected and then riveted. For supreme elegance, and more stately progress, one could turn to the teak-hulled *Swallow* of 1911, the perfect vessel for an Edwardian afternoon on Windermere, complete with tea made with the 'Windermere kettle', heated by the boiler. With a smaller engine, $4\frac{1}{2}$-, 6- and 8-inch cylinders, she travels at a more leisurely 10 knots. These and the other Windermere launches are delights, but the real virtues of the triple-expansion engine were to be seen in the mercantile fleet.

Left. Otto's *locomotive-style boiler*

Robin is one of that breed of dirty British coaster immortalised by Masefield. The conjunction of steam and screw propulsion was just moving into its second half-century when she was built in 1890 for the coastal traders, the Robin Steamship Company. Yet even at that late date the steamer shared the harbours with brigs and ketches, barquentines and topsail schooners – indeed, *Robin* was built 10 years before *Kathleen and May*. Visitors who see the two vessels at adjoining berths

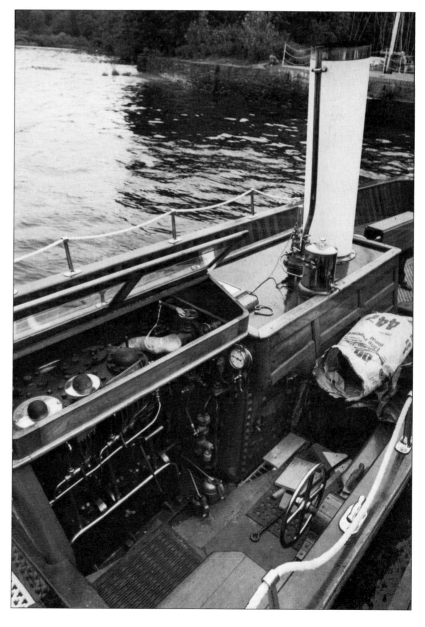

Swallow's *triple-expansion engine*

in St Katharine's Dock would probably think of the sailing vessel as being the elder of the two. If for no other reason, the proximity of the two old coasters does provide a useful lesson in maritime history. The 'new' steamer did not automatically oust the 'old' schooner. Nor are these two vessels necessarily of historical interest only, for there are signs in the shipping world that the coal-fired steamer and the commercial sailing vessel will have parts to play in an oil-starved future. It is, however, quite certain that whatever the new steamers and sail-assisted vessels turn out to be, they will not look very much like either *Robin* or *Kathleen and May*.

Robin is a steel-hulled vessel, 143 feet long, 23 feet wide with a draught of 13 feet. She was built by Thomson's of London and could carry a cargo of 400 tons, so that her carrying capacity is twice that of the neighbouring schooner. She has the classic lines of the nineteenth-century steamer. A number of early steamers survived for a long time, long enough at any rate to appear in photographs, so that we can see the similarities to say, *Collier*, built in 1848, or *John Bowes* of 1852. All are three-masted, with a tall thin funnel aft, the so-called Woodbine funnel, standing up like a thin fag, and a bridge forward of the funnel. There are many differences, of course, but the basic type is recognisably the same.

Robin is a robust craft, which remained in service until 1966, mostly working out of Spain, having been bought by a Spanish Company and renamed *Maria* in 1900. She was saved from scrap by the Maritime Trust and brought back to London. Her triple-expansion engines are by the famous firm of Gourlay Brothers of Dundee and are, in essence, the same as those of *Otto* and *Swallow* writ large. They still rely on connecting rods and crank to convert the up-and-down motion of the reciprocating engine into the rotating motion of the prop shaft. Four years after *Robin* was launched, a series of experiments culminated in the launching of a vessel driven by a quite different kind of engine.

The steam turbine uses steam pressure to drive a rotor directly. It was not a new idea. Hero of Alexandria developed such a machine in AD 50, and various inventors worked on the idea of applying the steam turbine to marine propulsion. The great Cornish engineer Richard Trevithick had a go in 1815, while James Cordes and Edward Locke of Newport, Monmouthshire, produced a highly successful model in 1846. None of these experiments was ever given practical application, and the first successful steam turbine did not appear until a good deal later. This was the work of Sir Charles Parsons.

When Parsons began his experiments he was not looking towards shipping at all, but searching for an efficient way of driving a dynamo for generating electricity. He realised that to try and use the total drop in steam pressure all in one stage to drive one huge rotor was hopelessly inefficient, the equivalent of the old one-cylinder engine. Instead, he proposed letting the pressure drop in stages, with a separate turbine at each stage. In 1884, he built a turbine for the Gateshead company of Clarke, Chapman, which consisted of a long shaft fitted with a series of blades, the rotor, set inside a case with fixed blades, the stator. High-pressure steam came in at one end and flowed along the horizontal axis, moving alternately between stator and rotor. In 1888, he designed the first ever turbo-powered generator for a power station, the Forth Banks Station of the Newcastle Electric Light Company. He continued to work on improving his power-station turbines and then, in the 1890s, turned his attention to the marine turbine.

Parsons began in 1894 by building a six-foot model of his proposed new vessel. The little boat, its propeller turned by rubber bands, was put through its paces on the pond at Heaton Works near Newcastle. From these experiments, he went on to build a launch, the *TY Turbinia*.

The marine turbine, first installed in the experimental steam yacht Turbinia

Turbinia *at speed in 1897*

Turbinia was built purely and simply as an experimental vessel, a hull to contain the Parsons turbine. She was built for speed, and seeing her today, preserved in the Science Museum in Newcastle-upon-Tyne, she looks the part. Her hull is 100 feet long, but at her widest she is a mere 9 feet across: she looks more like a missile than a ship. However, this is not quite *Turbinia* as she appeared on her first outing. At that time, she had a single turbine driving a single propeller. This original engine is in the Science Museum in London.

As with the power-station engines, the turbine works by passing steam alternately between rings of fixed and moving blades. These blades are set on discs, the discs increasing with size the further they are set from the steam inlet to allow for the expansion of the steam. The last two rotating discs have blades on both sides. The last disc also has blades fitted round the rim, which are moved by steam from a nozzle to make the vessel go astern.

Trials were a great disappointment. The engine was quite satisfactory, but the single propeller, moving at speed, carved great 'hollows' in the water, and the maximum speed was just over 20 knots. Parsons realised that what was needed was a greater surface area of propeller, so he took out the old engine and replaced it with what he called a

Stern view of Turbinia

Right. Turbinia's *propellers,*
three to each shaft

'parallel flow' engine. Instead of one turbine on one shaft, there were now three turbines, three shafts each carrying three propellers. Steam passed first to the high-pressure turbine on the starboard side, then to the intermediate on the port, and finally to a low-pressure turbine in the centre.

Steam was produced by a double-ended water-tube boiler, and extra heat was supplied by a fan which forced air through the fire. The steam left the boiler at a pressure of 210 p.s.i., which was reduced to 155 p.s.i. at the turbine inlet. The engine produced 2,000-shaft horse-power. At full speed, she must have been an amazing sight, but for those on board, trips were not without their hazards. Cleveland Moffat wrote an account of a trip in *Turbinia* which appeared in *Parson's Magazine* in 1898. With the fan going, flame shot from the funnel and red-hot cinders showered down, setting fire to the photographer's head-cloth. No run she ever made, however, could compare with the dash through the fleet at the Spithead Review of 1897.

Turbinia racing across the fleet at Spithead

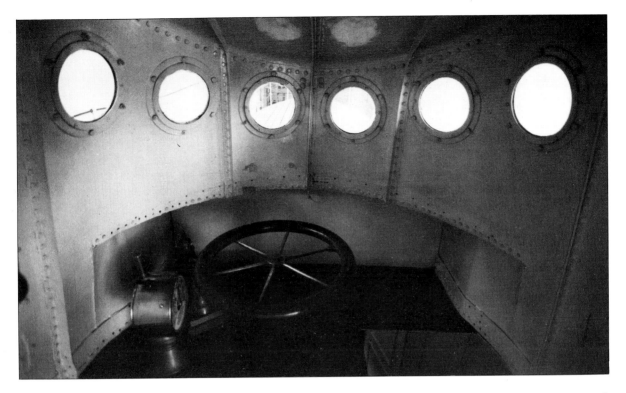

Turbinia's *wheel house*

Parsons saw the principal use of his engines as being in fast craft for the navy. The Admiralty were not noted for the enthusiasm with which they rushed to adopt new ideas, and Parsons saw Spithead as an opportunity to mount a demonstration that no one could ignore. The pride of the navy was on display that year, as part of the celebrations for Queen Victoria's Diamond Jubilee. In front of the great crowds, Parsons made his run at full speed, at the then undreamed-of rate of 34 knots. It was a sensation: no public relations man could have thought up a more dramatic advert for a new invention.

The run through the fleet became the subject of countless stories. It was claimed that Parsons had not received official permission for his eruption into the staid proceedings of the naval review, and that an infuriated admiral had sent his fastest craft to arrest the intruder. Needless to say, the admiral's launch never caught up. The story is delightful but untrue. But the true story needs no embellishment, for the demonstration was quite dramatic enough to leave no one in any doubt that there was a future for the steam turbine on the water.

It soon became obvious that while the direct drive was fine for the high-speed *Turbinia*, a much slower propeller speed was needed for larger, slower ships. Again Parsons pioneered this development, introducing reduction gearing on a small twin-screw launch in 1897. The toothed gears reduced the turbine speed of 20,000 r.p.m. to a propeller shaft turning at 1,400 r.p.m. This was still too fast for merchant ships, and a double-reduction gear had to be introduced. Soon the navy had a torpedo boat, *HMS Viper*, very much on the *Turbinia* pattern, which was recorded at just over 37 knots. In 1906 the first turbine battleship, *HMS Dreadnought*, put in an appearance. But perhaps the best known

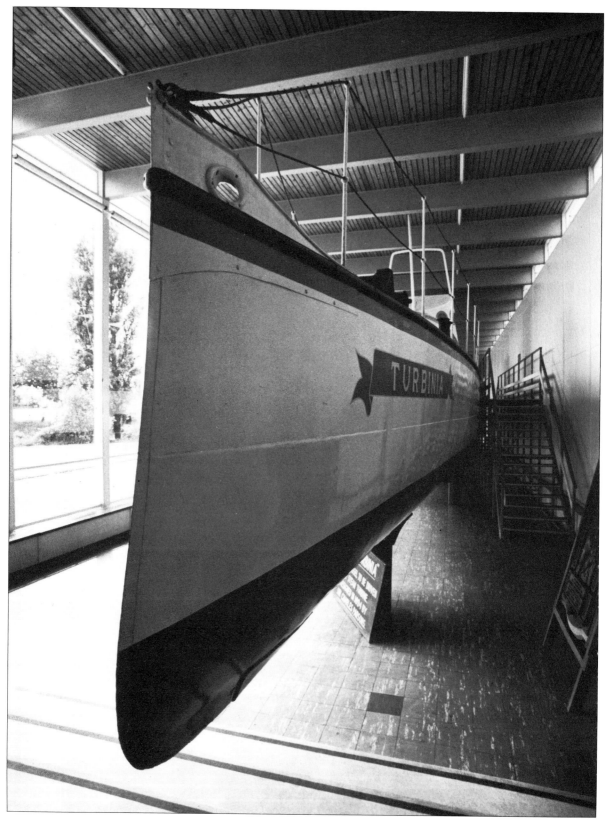

and best loved of all the vessels to be fitted with the new machinery were the great ocean liners which ran the Atlantic in the years before we took to the air.

The Cunard Liner *Mauritania* of 1906 showed the way. For 22 years she held the Blue Riband of the Atlantic for the fastest crossings. Then the 1930s saw the launching of some of the finest passenger liners ever built, including the magnificent French vessel, the *Normandie*, while Britain could boast two exceptional ships – the *Queen Mary*, launched in 1934, and the *Queen Elizabeth*, 4 years later. The *Queen Mary* had 2 turbines producing about 160,000-shaft horsepower and crossed the Atlantic in a record 3 days and 20 hours 40 minutes – something of an improvement over *Great Britain*'s 15 days. The *Queen Mary* held the riband until July 1952 when the American liner, the *United States*, carried off the prize on her maiden voyage. But the days of the great liners were almost over, and so were the days of steam. Shipbuilders looked to diesel and the gas turbine: passengers forsook the Atlantic liner for the Atlantic jet. The surviving liners turned to cruising.

The days of the steam-powered passenger liner may be over, but the steam-powered passenger ship is not yet dead. The Isle of Man Steam Packet Company ordered two vessels from Cammell Laird's of Birkenhead in the 1950s. *Mona's Isle* went out of service at the end of 1980, but her sister ship *Manxman* still carries on. She is not perhaps quite in the Queen class: where the *Queen Mary* weighed in with a gross tonnage of just over 80,000, *Manxman* seems almost a midget at 2,495 tons. But it is not just size that makes a Queen. The great Cunarders were noted for their elegance, and the same high standard of finish earned the two Manx boats the title of 'Little Cunarders'. The panelled rooms, the polished decks, the shining brass, add up to ships on which anyone would be proud to sail – even if the trip today is unlikely to take one further than Liverpool to Douglas or Llandudno. But it gives a taste of what the great days of ocean travel were like.

Manxman is by no means without interest in her own right. She was equipped with the latest thing in steam turbines, the Pametrada engine from Parsons and Metro Vickers. There are two engines, each of 4,500 horsepower, with double-reduction gearing, bringing propeller speeds down to 275 r.p.m. Unlike earlier vessels, *Manxman* is not coal-fired. The two water-tube boilers are heated by oil, and the steam is super-heated, that is to say, it is heated twice over, the second heating raising the temperature above 100°C to drive out any trace of water vapour.

One of the great advantages of steam is that once you have raised it, you can use it for all kinds of things besides just turning the engines. In *VIC 32*, steam could be led off to the deck-winch. Here it is used to help with steering the ship. A small engine is used to move the rudder, and *Manxman* is most unusual in that she has two rudders, one at each end. Being designed to work out of the narrow harbour at Douglas, it

The amazingly slender lines of a vessel built for speed

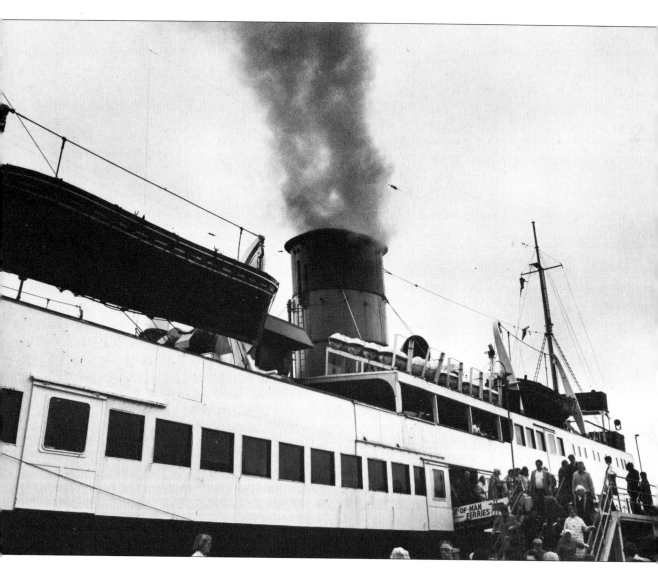

was a great help to have the bow rudder as well as the conventional stern rudder to aid in manœuvring, when going astern.

Manxman has the characteristics of a large vessel. For example, in little coasters like the Puffers, communication between captain and engineer was simplicity itself – they just shouted to each other down a speaking tube, and if the engineer had wandered off, the engine could still be worked through duplicate controls in the wheelhouse. In *Manxman*, communication between bridge and engine-room is by ship's telegraph, where signals rung up on the bridge are duplicated in the engine-room. Each system is appropriate to the particular needs of the particular vessel.

The passenger steamer Manxman

Manxman's *stylish*
dining saloon

5

The Silver Darlings

Fishing is one of man's oldest activities and, since at least late Saxon times, the British have gone to sea to follow the shoals of herring – the silver darlings. It was a vast trade. A hundred years ago, J. W. de Caux wrote a history of the herring fishery in which he estimated that at that time there were some 22,000 merchant vessels in Britain, but 30,000 fishing vessels. These were manned by more than 100,000 men and boys, while another 100,000 worked on shore in related trades. The fleets followed the herring shoals in their annual migrations. In winter and early spring, fishing was mainly in Irish waters, then it was off to Scotland for spring and summer and on down the English east coast in the autumn.

In England, the great centres for herring fishing were Lowestoft and Yarmouth. The latter was already recognised as a major port by the time of the Domesday Book, and in William I's time the tribute to be paid to the Abbey at St Edmond increased from 30,000 to 60,000 herring a year. In 1087, the Bishop of Norwich built a chapel and appointed a minister 'to pray for the health and prosperous success of the fishermen that come to fish at Yarmouth in the herring season'. A year later, the importance of Yarmouth was confirmed by the establishment of a Free Fair.

In 1357, the 'Statute of Herrings' was enacted, a document which gives an insight not only into the herring trade of the period but also into the fourteenth-century bureaucratic mind. Great Yarmouth having been designated a free port, the drafters of the Statute then proceeded to put limits on trade by a series of regulations: trading was limited to the time between sunrise and sunset, no fish could be sold at sea, no last of herring could be sold for a price in excess of 40 shillings, the price of carriage to London was fixed, and so on. The rules also specified that herring should be sold in hundreds, a 'hundred' being defined as one hundred and twenty herring, the fisherman's equivalent of a baker's dozen. Alongside the common white herring appeared the red herring – a smoked fish, ancestor of the mighty kipper, which proved irresistible to rats. A piece of red herring had only to be placed over a trap for the rat to walk blithely in, and this is how the phrase became synonymous with a false or misleading trail.

The British fishing industry received a formidable challenge in the fourteenth century, when the Dutch introduced a method of packing and salting herring at sea. Fishing was then no longer simply a local trade for small boats. The Dutch buss developed as a sturdy, round-hulled sailing vessel of up to a 100 tons, far larger than anything used by the British. The Scots reacted by banning Dutch vessels from their waters, which led to the war of 1532–41, forerunner of the twentieth-century cod war. The English continued to allow Dutch vessels in until the accession of James I, who came down from Scotland, bringing his restrictions with him. The days of the Free Fair at Yarmouth were over. They did not, however, keep the Dutch out of the fishing grounds

The Scottish Fisheries Museum at Anstruther

107

immediately outside territorial waters. By 1620, there were some 2,000 Dutch vessels in the North Sea, the biggest of them crewed by up to 15 men and boys. They could take as many as 100 lasts of herring, the last being a somewhat flexible measure, but then standing at 12,000 fish.

The British fleets continued for a long time to be composed almost entirely of small vessels, and in 1809 the government stepped in with active encouragement to the native industry, offering a bounty of £3 per ton to 'the owners of any whole-decked buss, or vessel, of not less than sixty tons burthern, being British-built, owned in Great Britain, and manned, navigated, and registered, according to law, which shall be fitted out for, and actively employed in, the deep sea British white herring fishery, on the coasts of Great Britain or Ireland'. There were other incentives to herring fishers, including a bounty paid on herring sold overseas. The result was a great expansion in the fishing fleets and the 1880s saw the volume of herring caught rise to the million-pound-a-year mark. Expansion, it seemed, could go on for ever. Yet even as early as 1881, de Caux was writing these words: 'The stern fact is, that the sea *is* exhaustible; and believing, as I do, that the great fish-farm round the British Isles should be worked with judgement as well as with skill, I invite attention to these matters.'

No one listened: the shoals were vast, and it seemed impossible to exhaust them. But the impossible happened, and the silver darlings have vanished. The herring that has been the main prey of the British fisherman for more than a thousand years has gone, killed off by over-fishing. When we look at other aspects of seafaring, we look at something which has a past, a present and a future. The herring fishery has only a past.

Rigging the small lugger Light. *The fish hold can be seen below decks*

There were two principal methods of fishing for herring – drifting and trawling. The former was very much the favoured method throughout history. In this method, the net is like a curtain hung in the water, into which the herring swim to be caught by the gills. In trawling, a large net is hauled along behind the boat, scooping up the fish and dragging them in. For a long time, any drifter had legal precedence over any trawler, so that the appearance of even one small drifter among a fleet of big trawlers was said to be rather like a sparrow-hawk popping up in a flock of sparrows.

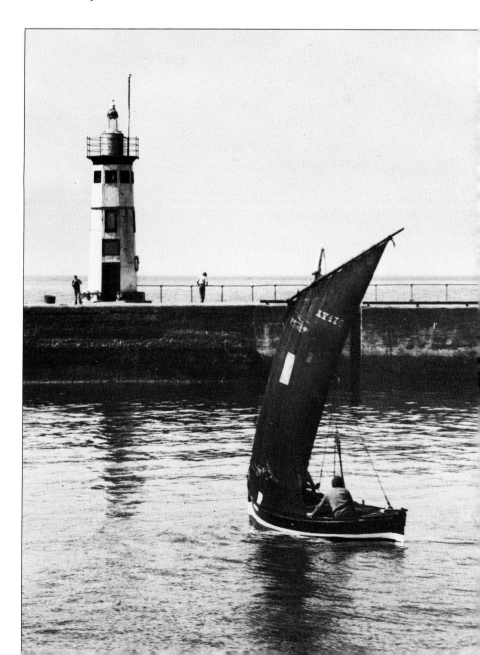

Light, *sailing in Anstruther harbour*

In this brief look at the deep-sea fishing industry, we shall be concentrating on the one main aspect, the herring drifter. One cannot, however, look at fishing only through boats and nets. It is an activity which involves the whole community, a point which is very strongly emphasised at the Scottish Fisheries Museum at Anstruther in Fife. The museum has two quite distinct elements, in more than one sense: there is a traditional museum in the village, based on buildings with long associations with the fishing trade, and there is a second part out on the waters of the harbour, in the shape of preserved craft.

When the history of Fife was written in 1710, Anstruther was described as being 'provided with all the accommodations for making and curing of herrings and which is the staple commodity of this town. . . . And this town sends about twenty-four boats to the fishing of herring.' Anstruther's history goes back beyond that. In the sixteenth century, the locals had used line-fishing with a long line carrying a multitude of baited hooks, and each boat had to supply the laird with 'a kylling and a fluke bannock', a cod and a turbot. When drift-net fishing came in, the east coast communities developed their own special craft – the fifie. It was originally an open boat, but by the middle of the nineteenth century it was decked over, and it is just such a decked fifie that can be seen afloat in Anstruther harbour.

The *Reaper* was built in 1901. Whereas early fifies were clinker-built, *Reaper* is carvel, but in spite of this one difference she still has the vertical stem- and stern-posts which are the distinctive features of her class. She has two masts, the forward of the two having a high dipping lugsail, rather like that on *Barnabas* (see p. 43), while the mizzen has a standing lug, that is, one which is not moved round the mast on tacking. The clew of the mizzen is attached to a boom on the stern. The decking is surrounded by an alarmingly low rail, which was no doubt a boon during fishing but did nothing to improve the safety of the vessel. Steering is by a wheel- and worm-screw to the rudder. The other principal feature above decks is a small capstan powered by a 12-horsepower steam-engine.

Reaper was actually used in the Shetlands, but small craft such as this regularly followed the shoals, even going as far south as Yarmouth for the English season. *Reaper* is 70 feet long with a 20-feet beam: her foremast is 65 feet high, the mizzen 55 feet, and with all sail spread she carries 3,000 square feet of canvas. At the time of writing, the museum was just completing the process of rerigging *Reaper* to bring her back to full sailing condition. The vessel itself might be restored, but that is not the same thing as restoration to a working condition, for the fishing boat is only really complete when fully fitted out for work. In her working days, *Reaper* would have carried over 40,000 square yards of netting, made up of 70 individual nets. To appreciate the special qualities of the fifie, you have to understand something of the way in which she was used.

Light *moored alongside the fifie* Reaper

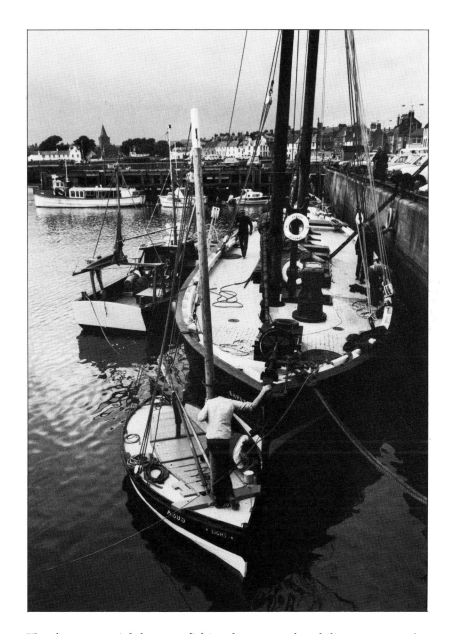

The first essential for any fishing boat was the ability to get to the fishing grounds at speed – and once there, to find and maintain a favourable position. When the skipper had selected his spot, the real work could begin.

There is more to fishing than heaving a net over the side and hoping. The drift-net is both big and complex. One starts with a basic cable, the warp, which is run out over the side of the vessel through a moveable pair of rollers known as the molgogger, which ensures the warp runs true. The warp slips below the surface, carrying the nets, attached by vertical lines or strops, with it. The top of the net is dotted with corks, which keep it about 12 feet below the surface, and its position is marked by canvas buoys. The fisherman ends up with a vertical curtain stretching for over a mile.

The fifie Reliance *at Great Yarmouth, nets and crew on board and ready for work*

Reaper putting to sea under power: but restorers hope to have her under sail again

When the skipper reached the spot where he had decided to fish, he put the vessel before the wind and the warp was run out through the molgogger. Two hands were given the job of managing the nets, while another took the strop-ropes as they came up on deck from the hold and passed them to the mate, who tied them to the warp. When the last of the 70 nets was in place, another 100 feet of warp was run out and the vessel was turned so that she was head-on to the wind. At this point, the foremast was lowered and the mizzen set to keep her on station. For the next 3 to 4 hours, the fifie drifted with the current while – or so the skipper hoped – the herring swam into the net. At the end of that time the hard work of hauling in the nets began.

The steam capstan, introduced in 1876, was used to help with raising and lowering the mainmast, but its chief job was to haul in the warp. As the warp came back on board, it was fed back down into the hold where a boy had the job of recoiling it, ready for the next trip. Up on the deck, often with the sea washing over and the boards made slippery by fish-scales, the men struggled with nets and fish. One man disconnected the strops and buoys, whilst the rest shook the fish from the net to slide away down the deck and through the hatches into the

Anstruther's zulu awaiting restoration

hold. When all was ready, sails were unfurled and the race was on to be first back to port to command the highest prices for the catch.

A fleet of fifies and zulus putting to sea

The fifie had originally replaced the older scaffie, a direct descendant of the old Viking craft. The fifie was a far sturdier vessel, but lacked something of the fineness of line which characterised its predecessor. In 1879, a fishing boat, the *Nonsuch*, was built which combined features of both scaffie and fifie. Instead of the vertical stern-post, there was a very steep rake to the stern. Masts and sails were made even larger, and the mainsail, with its very high peak, had no fewer than 6 rows of reef-points. Considering the problems of handling the lugsail, this was a massive sail, yet there were great advantages in keeping such an apparently cumbersome system in use. The small amount of rigging needed kept deck space clear for fishing, and with crews of at least 8 or 9, there were no manning problems. The tall foremast could easily be raised and lowered with the help of the capstan.

When *Nonsuch* was launched, Britain was heavily engaged in the Zulu Wars in Africa, and it was from these wars that the vessels got their name – the zulus. In time, the zulus were to be greatly changed, losing their mainsails and gaining a steam-engine instead. Anstruther's own zulu, the *Research*, berthed alongside *Reaper*, will eventually be refitted as a steam drifter. The change over to steam among the zulu fleets began around 1880, and the museum is fortunate in being able to show this important development. *Research* will not, however, be unique, for one other steam drifter has survived in England: the *Lydia Eva*.

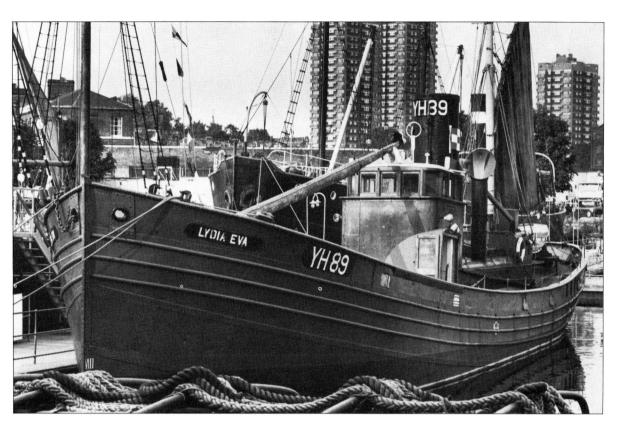

The Yarmouth steam drifter Lydia Eva *now berthed at St Katharine's Dock*

Lydia Eva worked out of the most important of all the herring fishing ports, Great Yarmouth. What strikes one immediately is the increase in scale over both the fifie and the zulu. *Lydia Eva* is 99 feet long with a 21-feet beam. She was built from the first as a steam drifter, rather than as an adaptation of a sailing boat, yet she is in many ways similar to the Scottish boats. The essential differences come in the hull, which is of steel not wood, but then that is no more than one would expect in a vessel built in 1930 – and in the power unit, a triple-expansion engine supplied with steam from a coal-fired scotch boiler. Steam is also used to power a generator to provide electricity for the boat – though in harbour, fuel was usually saved and the oil lamps had to be brought out again. In her working methods, however, she is virtually identical with the other boats. Nets were shot just as they were in the fifie and, when all was prepared, the steamer reverted to sail. A gaff-rigged sail on the mizzen was used, as the lugsail was on the fifie, to keep the drifter on station.

Although *Lydia Eva* was built primarily as a Yarmouth drifter, she was also fitted with a winch to enable her to serve as a trawler. Once there was a huge fleet of such vessels. In the bumper year of 1913, there were no fewer than 1,006 vessels fishing out of Yarmouth: 246 of them local, the rest down from Scotland. Between them, they landed 150,000 tons of herring, and another 80,000 tons at neighbouring Lowestoft.

Out of all that great fleet, only *Lydia Eva* – Yarmouth drifter YH 89 – has survived. She left East Anglia for her last voyage to a permanent berth in the Maritime Trust collection at St Katharine's in London.

Left. Lydia Eva *in her working days, leaving Great Yarmouth in the 1930s*

Right. *The speedboat* Otto *and its proud owners*

Below right. *The triple-expansion engine of the Windermere launch* Swallow

Below. *The engine-room on* Lydia Eva

Left. Manxman *in the Mersey*

Below left. *The fifie* Reaper *returning to Anstruther harbour*

While rejoicing that she has been preserved, one cannot help feeling that she has been taken out of her natural habitat. Fishing is about more than boats on the water, it is about whole communities. One can gain a glimpse into the significance of this by going back to the museum at Anstruther.

The buildings that house the collection are not only old but have a very long association with the fishing industry. In 1318, the Laird of Anstruther gave a parcel of land known as St Ayles land to the Abbey of Balmerino. Certain rights went with it, including the right to lease out booths to local fishermen, who were allowed to dry their nets on the land. A small community of fishermen developed, with a few coopers and brewers, and a chapel was built for them in the fifteenth century. Part of a window overlooking the museum courtyard is all that remains.

A century later, the Abbots Lodgings was built to provide a house for the Abbot and his retinue on their travels. This building now forms part of the museum. The other major building, opposite the Abbots Lodgings, is an eighteenth-century house, built for a local brewer, William Lumsden, who kept up an old tradition by recording the date of his marriage over the lintel of the outer door – 'WL–HD 1721'. Later the house became a ships' chandlers.

Reaper *moored at Anstruther, with the buildings of the Fisheries Museum behind her*

Throughout the museum, there are reminders of the time when this small area was busy with the activity of fishermen. In the courtyard are the 'gallowses' where the fishermen 'barked' their nets. To preserve the fabric, the nets were steeped in tanks of boiling water and oak bark, then hung up over the wooden gallowses to dry. There is another reminder of busier and earlier days in the museum door, which once belonged to the fish shed. Here the herring were packed away in barrels and each barrel was marked with a branding iron. The door carries a multitude of scars from where the irons were tested. So before one even begins to look at the exhibits proper in this splendid little museum, one has already received a short course in the history of fishing in Anstruther.

Fish barrel brands burned into the wooden door at the museum

The fisherman's house was partly home, partly workshop. In the eighteenth century, the typical cottage was single-storeyed, built, like so many other Scottish workers' cottages, but and ben. That is, there was a single, central entrance, with just two rooms, one on either side. The reconstructed cottage in the museum shows a house as it might have been at the end of the nineteenth century. Space is still very limited, but now there is an attic, a net loft where the gear was stored. It all helps to put the life of the fisherman in perspective, a reminder that however hard they worked at their dangerous trade, there were few fortunes to be made.

There are reminders, too, that in a fishing community it was not just the men who worked in the trade. In the days when fishing by line was commonplace, the women had the job of collecting the live bait and fastening it to the thousand or more hooks that made up a line. Later, when drift-net fishing became almost universal, the 'lassies' had the job of gutting and packing the herring. They worked at an astonishing speed, and their work was not limited to helping out in the home port. They, too, followed the migration of the herring from Yarmouth in the south to the Shetlands in the north. Often living conditions were primitive in the extreme. On the Shetlands, they lived in huts, sleeping three to a bed and with no furniture apart from the communal table and their own travelling boxes, which served them for seats. Not that much furniture was needed, for there was little enough time for sitting around and chatting.

A whole cluster of other tradesmen depended on the fishermen – fish buyers, carters who took the fish from the ports, net menders, boat builders, coopers who made the barrels for the fish, and so on. It was estimated that for every drifter that went to sea at the end of the nineteenth century there were a hundred individuals whose livelihood depended on it.

In many ways the fishing community of that time was similar to the mining community. Whole families were involved, sons following fathers into the trade, with the women at work, picking and sorting coal in one case, gutting and packing fish in the other. Both were closed communities, brought together by shared work and shared dangers.

One result of a community living close to danger is the growth of a great catalogue of superstitions, many of which bear no apparent relation to the threat or promise they represent. Certain words could never be used. One can see that it might be tempting providence to refer to a 'good catch', but why on earth should there be a taboo on 'pig' and 'rabbit'? And why did a Scots fisherman never cut his finger nails on a Tuesday?

Many of the superstitions related to the church. In Yarmouth, if a fisherman saw a nun on the way to his boat, he would shout 'iron, iron' and run to touch something made out of that metal. There were some beliefs that did contain an element of logic, such as throwing money

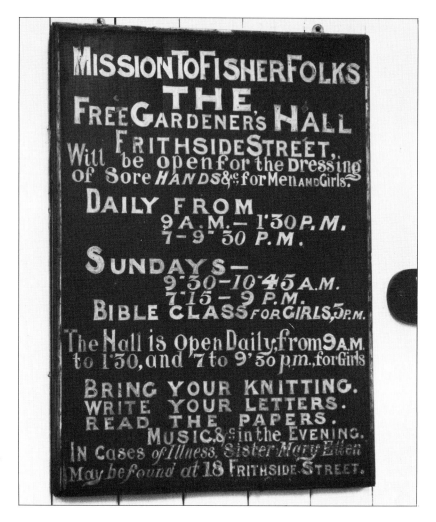

Notice preserved in the museum at Anstruther

overboard to 'buy a catch'. It is striking, though, how few of the charms are intended to bring good luck, and how many to ward off misfortune. And the bad omens were taken very seriously indeed; so much so that a man would rather lose a day's good fishing than take to sea after he had seen a rat leaving his boat.

Misfortune was too common not to be taken seriously. The fishing community round Anstruther has had its share of tragedy. Perhaps the worst was in 1875, when there was a violent storm in which 5 local boats went down with the loss of 37 lives. But such danger does not belong solely to the comparatively remote past. Recently local fishermen asked the museum staff at Anstruther if space could be found in a quiet corner for a memorial room, with plaques to commemorate those who have died at sea in the years since the Second World War. There are, sadly, many plaques on that wall. Fishing is still a hazardous business, and it is because they themselves have suffered so much that the fishing community has played such a big part in helping to save life at sea.

The idea of a specialist lifeboat service is a comparatively modern one. Until late in the eighteenth century, the saving of life at sea was closely allied to the business of salvage. Small boats would put out to a wreck with the hope of grabbing a share of a possible valuable cargo; rescuing the crew would often take second place. This is, of course, a generalisation covering a huge range of human motives and actions. At one end of the scale were the notorious wreckers who deliberately lured ships to their doom; at the other there were always some who were ready to risk their lives to save others. In between, no doubt, was a much larger group, who went out to wrecks for what they could get but at the same time, made every effort to help survivors. Local fishermen from Deal and Walmer, for example, have a long history of salvaging cargoes as well as saving lives from vessels that foundered on the Goodwin Sands. The boats they used were the boats they normally used for fishing, with no special adaptations.

In 1786, a London coachbuilder, Lionel Lukin, came up to the north-east with the idea for what he called an 'unimmergible', an unsinkable lifeboat. His ideas were tried out and proved quite successful. A local fishing boat, a coble, was adapted and did good service, but it was no more than an adaptation of an existing craft. The first purpose-built lifeboat was the *Original*, which came into being after a Newcastle tragedy four years later.

In September 1790, a Newcastle ship, the *Adventurer*, was wrecked off the mouth of the Tyne. She was in sight of land, but the heavy seas prevented anyone on the shore from reaching her: the watchers could do nothing but stand there as the ship broke up and the crew drowned. A local society decided something should be done, and placed the following advertisement in the Newcastle papers:

A Reward of Two Guineas will be given to any Person producing a PLAN (which shall be approved by the Committee appointed for that Purpose as the Best) of a Boat, capable of containing 24 Persons, and calculated to go through a very shoal, heavy, broken Sea: The Intention of it being to preserve the Lives of Seamen, from Ships coming ashore, in hard Gales of Wind.

William Wouldhave, the parish clerk of South Shields, produced a winning design, but the committee was not convinced that it met all the requirements they had specified, so they gave him one guinea rather than two and entrusted the job of incorporating his ideas into a better design to the local boat builder, Henry Greathead. The result was the *Original*, launched in 1790. Altogether, Greathead built another 31 of these vessels, one of which, the *Zetland*, built in 1800, has survived, and is housed in its own small museum overlooking the sea at Redcar.

The oldest surviving lifeboat, Zetland

Left. *The* Zetland *preserved in her own museum at Redcar*

The *Zetland* is a clinker-built vessel, 30 feet long, looking in profile rather like a slice of melon, with a pronounced upward curve at stem and stern. She owes much of her design to the fishing boats that worked off the beaches of north-east England. She was given extra buoyancy by the addition of cork fenders and buoyancy chambers, and she was moved through the water by means of 5 pairs of oars. Steering was by means of a pair of long steering-oars set in the stern. She was kept mounted on a wheeled trolley, so that she could be launched off the open beach. She looks decidedly primitive, but she had a long and successful working life, going out to her last rescue in 1880.

Over the years, there have been many improvements in lifeboat design. At first, development was slow but a great advance was made in the 1820s with the establishment of the Royal National Lifeboat Institution, a volunteer organisation founded by Sir William Hillary to control lifeboats all round the English coast, a job it still does today. The biggest change in the nineteenth century came with the introduction of various kinds of self-righting lifeboats. These had what we now think of as the classic lifeboat shape, with high-rising buoyancy compartments at bow and stern. They were still pulling-and-sailing lifeboats – that is, they were moved by both oars and sail. Steam power was introduced in 1890, to be followed by the internal combustion engine, but it was not until 1950 that the last pulling lifeboat went out of service, marking the end of the line of vessels started by Lukin and Greathead. The other tradition, that of the fishermen who volunteer for the dangerous work of the lifeboatman, has never been broken.

6 *Wooden Walls*

Special boats for special purposes: the fishing boat is an obvious example, the warship would seem to be another. Yet this was not always so. The warship was at first thought of as simply a means of bringing armed men to attack the enemy, generally on land but sometimes on an enemy vessel. Gunpowder changed all that. With cannon on board, the sea battle could be fought at a distance – not, at first, a very great distance, but nevertheless warring vessels did not have to make physical contact, except for boarding to take a prize.

A new generation of ships had to be developed that could take a large quantity of armament yet which would still be swift and manoeuvrable. The latter was especially important as, in a fleet engagement, position was vital: the fleet stationed to windward had an automatic advantage in being able to sail at the enemy and dictate tactics. They might not win the battle, but they could at least determine the way in which it would be fought, much as white can dictate the opening moves in a game of chess. Producing the ideal, fast, manoeuvrable and well-armed warship was the work of the ship designers.

The wooden walls of the eighteenth century were the direct descendants of the galleons and other ships which had fought the Spanish in the days of Drake, Raleigh and Hawkins. Hawkins introduced a basic shape to the hull which was to set the pattern for the next century and a half. Earlier vessels had been very high at bow and stern and very low in the waist. Hawkins's ship had a pronounced poop at the stern but the fo'c'sle in the bows was scarcely raised above deck level. This helped to make the ship much more manoeuvrable. It could sail far closer to the wind because the vessel's tendency to drift to leewards was greatly reduced. Speed was dependent on shape of the hull both above and below the water-line, and here designers had to cope with two conflicting requirements. The best speed comes when a vessel is slender, with fine lines, able to slice easily through the water: but what the gunners wanted was a wide vessel to supply a solid platform for their cannon.

Battles were mainly fought by fleets facing each other in parallel lines, firing broadsides. The cannon were lined up along the sides of the vessels, and they needed a great deal of space to allow for recoil after firing. A special hull shape was developed, which tapered quite sharply down towards the keel to give good underwater lines, bulged out above the water-line where the guns were set and then, so as not to make the whole thing top-heavy, curved in again towards the upper deck, which carried little or no armament. This type of curve to the hull is known as the tumblehome.

The stout walls of these vessels provided stalwart defence against enemy shot – but the vessels were vulnerable at stem and stern. The old, square stern was often very beautiful, with galleries of windows and ornate decoration, but there was no protection to shot, which could go straight down the length of the deck and cause utter havoc.

The wooden walls of HMS *Victory*

127

The most devastating of all manœuvres was that in which a vessel was able to rake the stern of the enemy, sailing across behind her, while each gun in turn fired into that vulnerable area. The bow, with its long projecting beak, was almost equally vulnerable. During the eighteenth century, both stem and stern became more rounded, which meant that extra armament could be added to protect both ends of the ship.

Change was not limited to the hull. Perhaps the most important innovation which affected warships much as it had affected merchant ships, was the change from tiller and whipstaff to steering-wheel. This gave far greater control to the vessel and made for much more accurate manœuvring. And because the ship was now handier in its steering, it made sense to move towards a more sophisticated sail pattern that would enhance the captain's control still further. The ship may have been in essentials the three-masted ship of Armada days, but the addition of triangular jibsails on the bowsprit and staysails between the masts, together with the cutting down of the old lateen sail on the mizzen, so that it became, in effect, a type of gaffsail, brought many of the advantages of the fore and aft rig to the basic square-rig design. The new sails enabled the captain to go closer to the wind, eliminating miles of tacking. Though the ship might not be moving faster through the water, she would be getting to her destination sooner, which was what mattered.

The large warships of the eighteenth century required vast quantities of timber, so the independent shipbuilders who served the navy established their yards close to heavily forested regions. One example is Buckler's Hard on the Beaulieu River, south of the New Forest. It was here that such notable vessels as *Agamemnon*, a 64-gun vessel, said to have been Nelson's favourite command, were built. Today Buckler's Hard has a maritime museum and the little village has been preserved much as it was two centuries ago.

The modern visitor might be surprised at the lack of evidence that anything larger than a rowing boat has ever been built at Buckler's Hard. It has none of the features one associates with a modern yard – no dry docks, no cranes, no covered slipway, just a wide, main street running down to the water's edge. One might guess that this is because all the evidence of shipbuilding has been destroyed, but in fact an eighteenth-century shipbuilder would be quite happy to turn up at Buckler's Hard even now and set about gathering in the materials to start building. If we look at how he would have carried out his task, we can see that there was never really any physical evidence to destroy.

The first stage in constructing a naval ship was the preparation of drawings and, from the drawings, a model and, from that, templates in the mould loft – the process already described in Chapter Three. The mould loft had no special characteristics to distinguish it from other simple buildings. The major part of the work went on out in the open. Launchways were cut at right angles to the river bank and here the

The main street at Buckler's Hard, leading down to the Beaulieu River

All that remains of the slipways where ships were built for Nelson's navy

ship itself was built. First the keel was laid down with the supporting keelson above it. Stem- and stern-posts were added, frames positioned in between. Knees held the decking and the strengthening beams. Planking was added to the outside. Greater strength was provided in late eighteenth-century vessels by the construction of a double hull, planking both inside and outside the skeleton frame.

All this required not only vast quantities but many different kinds of timber. Elm was generally used for the keel – as many as seven large pieces being scarfed together in a large vessel. Fir, spruce and pine, mostly imported from the Baltic, were used for masts and spars – as much as half a mile of timber in the biggest warships. But far and away the largest quantity went into the frame, and here the old phrase about British warships having hearts of oak is found to be based on fact. It was English oak that provided the main timber for the frames. It had one great advantage over all other wood: it could supply 'compass' timber of the right size and strength. The knees, curved timber pieces that were fitted to the vertical wall and then bent round to support the horizontal beams, had to come from a single piece so that the grain ran true. The oak, with its thick branches standing at right-angles to the trunk, was ideal. But only trees, at least a century old, were suitable.

The destruction of timber was on a massive scale. It was measured in 'loads', a single load being the amount one horse could pull in a cart, generally about a ton. A ship like *Agamemnon* needed 2,000 loads of timber. No wonder that the number of loads in the New Forest fell from an estimated 115,000 at the beginning of the seventeenth century to just over 30,000 at the end of the eighteenth. The visitor to Buckler's Hard two centuries ago would have found a scene dominated by two impressive sights: one or more ships slowly growing on the launch-ways, and around the whole area, great piles of timber slowly season-ing in the open air. Shipbuilding was not a hurried occupation: when a major ship was needed, timber had to be cut literally years before work began. Now the ships have all been launched, the stocks of timber have long gone and only traces of the launchways remain.

The eighteenth-century shipbuilding firm depended for its success on the skill of the individual master builder. As a result, firms came, enjoyed a brief, flourishing period, and then, as quickly, could fade back into obscurity. Shipbuilding centres found their importance tied very much to the firms who worked there, so that they too flourished and faded.

Buckler's Hard was in fact never intended as a shipbuilding centre: it came about through an accident of history. In 1709, the Duke of Montagu decided to create a major port on the Beaulieu River for the importation of colonial produce. In order to import the produce, he needed a colony, so an expedition was fitted out and sent to establish a base at St Lucia. Unfortunately for the Duke's plans and the £10,000 he had invested in the enterprise, the expedition had barely settled in

Buckler's Hard as it appeared in 1803, with Swiftsure *and* Euryalus *being built. The model is in the maritime museum*

when news reached them that the island had been annexed by France, and they were all promptly sent packing. In the meantime, the Duke had begun laying out Montagu Town, starting with an impressive main street, 80 feet wide, flanked by brick houses. And that was as far as it ever got. With no produce there was no port, but the geography of the new town, on a deep-water river, surrounded by timber and with a broad street down to the water, made it ideal for shipbuilding. Montagu Town became Buckler's Hard, and a succession of ship-builders leased the site, the most famous and successful being Henry Adams, who was there from 1747 until his death in 1805.

The fortunes of those who built ships for the navy rose and fell with the changing tides of foreign affairs. Peace meant an empty order book: war and the threat of war brought work in plenty. One of the most active periods at Buckler's Hard coincided with the American War of Independence, a disastrous conflict for most of Britain, but good news for navy suppliers. It was at this period that *Agamemnon*, one of the biggest, and certainly the most famous, of all the ships to be built at Bucklers Hard, was ordered. As was normal practice, only the basic hull was completed here, after which she went for fitting out at Portsmouth.

That she was Nelson's favourite ship says much for the skills of *Agamemnon*'s builder. In those days, the master shipbuilder was a combination of artist, engineer, carpenter and organiser. There is ample evidence of Adams' skill in the first category, for some of his sketchbooks have survived. These are more than mere sketches of ships either out on the water or floating through the artist's imagination: they are the essential starting point for new designs. The ship was seen first as a complete entity before anything approximating to a detailed drawing was produced. Adams' vision gave the ship its shape, and his was very much the controlling hand throughout construction. Even after he was supposed to have retired, he kept a close watch on the business. When times were hard, as in the 1790s, Henry Adams, then 80, got on his horse and rode up to London to drum up work for his sons. His house still stands, and in the latter years of his life he had his own little eyrie at the top of the house, from which he could watch the work through a telescope. Every man on the workforce had a number, and if Henry Adams saw anything amiss a bell was rung and the man's number hoisted at the flagpole. The miscreant worker then had to climb a ladder to receive a dressing down from his old master. It was a small, closely controlled community, which prospered when the ships they created prospered.

Shipbuilders were notoriously secretive about their art. The secret might turn out to be no more than a man having a good eye for a ship's line, but was no less jealously guarded for all that. It was not, however, an attitude that was conducive to improvements in design. One of the most famous contemporary books on the subject, William Falconer's *New Dictionary of the Marine*, had this to say on the subject: 'Nothing appears more effectually to have retarded the progress of naval architecture, than the involving [of] it in mysteries which the professors would gravely insinuate are only intelligible to themselves. This ridiculous affectation is, nevertheless, too generally retained.' Secretive Adams and his colleagues may have been, but they built some of the finest ships of the age, though not the biggest.

In the middle of the eighteenth century, Admiral Anson introduced a system by which ships were rated according to the number of guns they carried.

First Rate	100 guns or more
Second	84–100 guns
Third	70–84 guns
Fourth	50–70 guns
Fifth	32–50 guns
Sixth	less than 32 guns

Only the first 3 rates were considered ships of the line, able to take their place in the line of battle for the war of the broadsides. The first-rate ship was not necessarily better than the second-rate, simply larger. Many of the smaller vessels, fourth-rate and below, were frigates, the eyes of the fleet, fast vessels that hunted out the enemy then raced back with their reports. The first-rates were built at the great naval dockyards, and there is now one sole survivor, *HMS Victory*.

The *Victory* has survived because of her associations with one of Britain's greatest sailors, Nelson, and one of her greatest naval successes, Trafalgar. In a way this is unfortunate, for the interest in the Nelson connection has deflected attention from the ship itself. In fact,

The upper deck of Victory

when the battle of Trafalgar was fought in 1805, *Victory* was already quite an elderly lady by navy standards, and had received more face-lifts than an ageing Hollywood actress. When we see *Victory* today, resplendent in her dry dock at Portsmouth, we are seeing her as she was at just one moment in her very long history.

The *Victory* story really begins in 1758, when Pitt persuaded Parliament that naval strength had been reduced too far for safety, and 12 new ships of the line were ordered, headed by a 100-gun first-rater. There were only four first-rate ships in the navy at that time, and the design for the newcomer was based on the most successful ship of the day, the *Royal George*, launched in 1756, and accepted as having quite exceptionally good sailing characteristics for a big ship of that time.

Victory was designed by Sir Thomas Slade, the Senior Surveyor to the navy. In June 1759, details of her size and proposed armament were first published: length on the gun deck, 186 feet, length of the keel, 151 feet 3½ inches, extreme breadth, 51 feet 10 inches. The guns were arranged so that the heaviest came at the widest part of the vessel, close to the water-line – thirty 42-pounders on the lower deck, twenty-eight 24-pounders on the middle, thirty 12-pounders on the upper, with ten 6-pounders on the after-deck and two 6-pounders on the fo'c'sle. Work was put in hand at the Chatham dockyard, which then employed 1,300 men, on whom 640 were shipwrights. All was urgency – then the Peace of Paris was signed in 1762, work slowed down and men were laid off. It was not until 1765 that the new first-rater, which had already been given her official name of *Victory*, was finally floated. She was to enjoy a long and eventful career.

In 1778, she put to sea for the first time and immediately went into active service as Keppel's flagship. In 1780, her armament was greatly improved by the addition of two 24-pounder carronades. These were comparatively short, wide-bored cannon, so named because they were first cast at the Carron Ironworks in Scotland. Britain's industrial revolution was now well underway, yet this was the only area which was seriously touched by change as far as the navy was concerned. The new-style foundries, on the pattern set by Abraham Darby at the beginning of the century, were not just turning out more iron than ever before, they were also able to produce large castings of high quality. A French brigadier, visiting Britain in 1773, was very impressed particularly by the improvements to naval guns. He pointed out, in a report to the French government, that since the introduction of the new system of casting, not a single British naval cannon had exploded, whereas in France accidents were so common that French sailors were said to be more afraid of their own guns than of the enemy's. The carronade was not only larger and safer than other cannon, it was more accurate. Naval gunnery was then a complex business, but it was far from being an exact science.

A gun crew could consist of as many as 15 men for the largest weapons. The gun was loaded by ladling in a charge of powder equal to a third of the weight of the shot. Then a wad of rope-yarn was rammed home, followed by the ball and another wad of yarn. After this the gun was primed by filling the touch-hole with powder, which could then be lit for firing. The gun had first to be positioned by the gun captain. It could be elevated and depressed by using a hand-spike as a

Right. *The gun deck of* Victory

Below right. Unicorn's *figurehead*

The ward room of Victory

Left. *Inside a six-inch gun turret on* HMS Belfast

Below left. *The control room and periscope of the submarine* Alliance

One of Victory's *great capstans*

lever, then held in position by a wedge. Here the carronade was a great improvement, for it was fitted with a screw to elevate it, giving much finer control than was possible with the spike. Tackle was used to move the gun horizontally. So there was some movement in all directions, up and down, and side to side.

There was, however, a further complication, for the ship was also moving, and the stability of the ship played an important part in good gunnery. It was the gun captain's job to choose the precise moment of firing – and different nationalities had their own views on the best place to aim. The French preferred to aim when the ship was rising, so that the ball went high towards the enemy's spars and rigging. The Americans fired on the fall, hoping to pierce the enemy's hull. The British, ever masters of compromise, went in between, firing when the ship was on an even keel.

When all was ready, the gun captain pulled the lanyard attached to the flint lock, the powder was ignited and the gun fired. As it fired, the gun crew released the side-tackles and the gun recoiled backwards for as much as eleven feet. The type of shot varied. There was cannon ball, which could sink the enemy, assuring victory but depriving the victors of a valuable prize; chain-shot to slash through sails and rigging and damage spars; and grape-shot to attack the crew. One outstanding feature of the British ship of the line was the efficiency of the gun crew who, according to one contemporary account, were able to get in three broadsides to the enemy's one. This was probably an exaggeration. Nevertheless, the British gun crews did have considerable expertise – partly because of assiduous practice, and partly because the slow match, a smouldering rope-end, had been replaced by the flintlock as the means of firing.

The gun decks were the essential parts of the ship. It was for gunnery that the ship existed, and when changes were made it was usually with the aim of increasing the effectiveness of the fire-power. However, safety was another element: there was little point in bringing up your guns if you yourself were liable to be blown out of the water by a single shot. So magazines were kept below the water-line for safety, but as close to the guns as possible, and were hung up to allow air to circulate to keep them cool. Other improvements were made to *Victory* to affect her sailing characteristics and general seaworthiness, such as having her bottom coppered.

Then, in 1797, *Victory* was demoted to the lowly status of hospital ship and was nearly reduced to the ultimate indignity of becoming a prison hulk. Voices were raised on her behalf, probably Nelson's among them. She was too good a ship to be lost to active service, so a 'middling' refit was ordered. It is reassuring to discover that military cost estimates were no more accurate then than now: the estimated cost was £23,500 and the actual cost £70,933, rather more than the hull cost to build in the first place. The most obvious alteration was to the stern, which was given the new rounded form. She had two more refits before sailing off in 1805. She was given two 68-pound carronades on the fo'c'sle, thirty 32-pounders on the lower deck, twenty-eight 24-pounders on the middle, thirty 12-pounders on the upper deck, twelve 12-pounders on the quarter deck and two more on the fo'c'sle – quite an increase in armament since her first launch. This was her condition as she sailed away to war to take her place in the Battle of Trafalgar.

It is because of her role at Trafalgar that *Victory*, the last of the first-raters, has been saved. To describe her as having been preserved would be slightly misleading, since it suggests that we see her today as she was when she returned from battle. Severely damaged at Trafalgar, at first she was relegated to a second-rater, then put on permanent stationary duty until by the beginning of this century she was little more than a rotting hull.

In 1922, thanks to a massive fund-raising exercise, *Victory* was at last lifted out of the water into her new permanent home in No. 2 Dock, Portsmouth. It was then possible to see how badly the old ship had suffered: there were holes in the side you could actually walk through. She was a very different creature from the vessel that had led the fleet at Trafalgar. The decision was taken to restore her, so that she would look as she did on that day. This involved considerable rebuilding, including the removal of many heavy guns. The massive wooden masts had already gone, and she was rerigged with lighter, metal replicas to reduce the load for her new life out of the water. Purists might argue that her reincarnation is largely a fake. Perhaps so, but it is an exceptionally good one, which allows every opportunity to study the special characteristics of the warship of the past.

Just as in the case of the small luggers, the demands of fishing ensured that there were always enough hands to man the vessel under sail, so the gun crews ensured a more than adequate complement. There were, in fact 850 officers and men on board. Manpower was quite definitely not a problem when it came to sailing *Victory*, so there was no need either to restrict the size and number of sails or to go to any great lengths to reduce handling difficulties. The spread of sail was immense. Though there is no sail carried at present, the size of masts and yards gives a good idea of what she would have been like under sail. The mainmast, for example, measures 203 feet from truck to water-line, and the main yard is 102 feet 4 inches long. The yard could be extended even further by booms to take extra sail – the studding sails or stunsails – added to make the most of light breezes.

Lack of machinery could be compensated for by weight of numbers. Take, for example, the use of a capstan to break an anchor clear from the bottom. There are two capstans, each with two barrels, one on the middle gun deck and another, on the same shaft, on the deck below. Twenty-six bars were inserted and 10 sailors manned each bar – 260 men in all. The capstans also served as first-aid posts during battle, when a packet of salt for rubbing into wounds, and a piece of canvas for a makeshift bandage, were kept in the bar sockets.

The massive wooden knees that accounted for so much of the timber aboard Victory

Another feature of *Victory* is the almost complete absence of metal in the overall construction. Wrought-iron bolts, often several feet long, held timbers together, though wooden treenails were even more extensively used. Yet the main structures were still massive pieces of wood, even though by the time of Trafalgar the industrial revolution had entered a new phase of development, and the first steam locomotive had already plodded, asthmatically wheezing, down its iron road. It was to be some time yet before steam power reached the navy, but the use of iron to replace wood in the structure of ships could not be long delayed. Anxiety over timber supplies had led to huge new plantations being started in the eighteenth century, but the trees had to mature, and by that time they were no longer to be needed. Ships might still use wooden planking for the hull, but that never represented a major part of the wood used. The frame took 70 per cent of the timber, and it was the curved compass timber from mature trees that was the first to be replaced. It represented a huge stock of wood. *Victory*, for example, has 438 knees, all of oak. Replace those by metal and you had a huge saving in timber.

Falconer, in his *New Dictionary* of 1815, recorded that 'Mr Thomas Roberts of the Navy-office, had lately succeeded in the invention of a method of securing the beams of ships to their sides': he used iron knees. In 1807, he was awarded £800 by the King's Order in Council and the Society of Arts gave him their silver medal. Outwardly the new ships, built with the new technology, might seem much the same as their forerunners, but inside the differences are plain. They can be observed in *HMS Unicorn*, the oldest British ship still afloat.

Unicorn was built at Chatham in 1824 and represents a fascinating halfway stage between the wooden ship *Victory* and the iron and steel ships that were to come. She has survived so long not because, like *Victory*, she took part in a famous battle, but for the contrary reason that she never saw service at sea at all. Perhaps because we can look at her with a vision unclouded by the romantic mists which surround a vessel that has seen great days, we can get from *Unicorn* a very clear picture of life in the last days of the wooden walls.

Unicorn was, in fact, never completed. Britain fought no naval wars, so no new battleships were needed. For a long time this vessel, designed as a speedy frigate, did nothing at all but sit at anchor doing service as a store-ship. When she was finally moved, it was only to be taken under tow to Dundee in 1873. It is there that she has her home, and there, it is hoped, that *Unicorn* will finally emerge as the vessel her designers always intended her to be. At present, she is little more than a hull with an odd sort of housing on top, reflecting her recent role as training ship for the Royal Navy Reserves. Even so, one can see at first glance that this is a vessel built on very different lines from the first-rate ship. There is still a tumblehome, but far less pronounced than in *Victory*. Altogether, the lines are much finer with a sharp point to the

Unicorn's *hull, with the roof that was installed shortly after launching*

bows. She looks what she was, a vessel designed for speed, yet heavily armed with 42 guns, consisting of 18-pounders and 32-pound carronades. The frigate had come a long way from the time when it was simply thought of as a messenger ship.

Unicorn was large, over a thousand tons, about half the size of *Victory*: the nineteenth-century equivalent of the twentieth-century cruiser. She carried her armament all the way round, even into the captain's cabin in the stern. The captain might enjoy the luxury of a cabin to himself, but when battle stations were called, his furniture and belongings were bundled out of the way to make room for the gun crews. That, however, was something no captain of the *Unicorn* has ever had to face.

Once inside the vessel one can see just how different the design is from that of the previous century. The iron knees, joining sides to beams, look scarcely more substantial than the brackets holding up the bookshelf at home. This combination of lightness and strength was of course the great attraction to shipbuilders. Just as important as the knees were the iron bands which ran diagonally across the planking to reinforce the hull. *Unicorn* is something more than a halfway point between the wooden ship and the iron ship. Just as sail and steam existed together for more than a century, so the navy kept wooden hulls long after the first successful mercantile iron ships had proved their worth. There were good reasons for this, as we shall see in the next chapter. It was the need to stay with wooden ships that made the changes in framing so important.

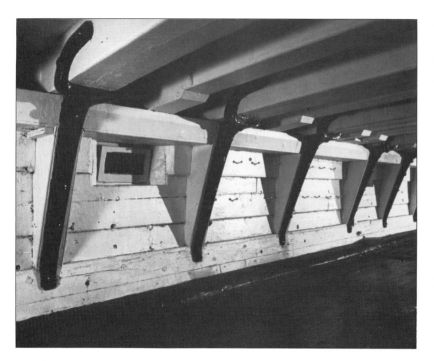

The nineteenth-century answer to eighteenth-century timber shortages – iron knees on Unicorn

Below. *Restricted head room is very much a feature of the frigate: the ward room with officers' cabins behind the louvred doors*

Below decks, *Unicorn* provides a fascinating insight into the condition under which officers and men worked in the wooden frigate. Moving around the ship is rather like trying to walk in a coal-mine, for there is so little space between decks that everything has to be done at the stoop. The crew's quarters were on the lower deck, a dark, airless, cramped space where 180 men slung their hammocks, and where bumps on the head were so common that an eminent naval surgeon, Sir Gilbert Blase, put forward the theory that it was this that accounted for the high incidence of lunacy among sailors. The men occupied about half the lower deck, and there was a company of marines separating them from the 'luxury' of the officers' quarters, as a protection against mutiny, not an entirely unknown phenomenon in the navy at that time.

The officers' quarters were not, in fact, very much better than the men's. There was a wardroom where they relaxed and ate, lined on either side by minute cabins, closed off by louvred doors to provide some ventilation. The cabin furnishings were strictly graded by rank, with crude bunks for the junior officers. The captain's cabin on the deck above, light and airy with windows set into the stern, representing pure luxury by comparison.

Unicorn's upper deck presents a somewhat misleading impression, being roofed in where once it would have been open to the skies. Even here, however, something of the modernity of the vessel can be seen in the big double steering-wheel, while the attractive lines are more plainly revealed on a deck that is not encumbered with masts and rigging. Apart from her importance in the story of naval technology, *Unicorn* has another less easily defined attraction. She has about her an indefinable atmosphere, the sense of being a living, working ship, which is even stranger when one considers that she has never served at sea. Certainly there can be few vessels where one feels more conscious of the special nature of the seafaring life, of the closed community deprived of all but the most rudimentary of facilities. Four hundred men, for example, had to share just 4 toilets, and those were out on the beak at the head of the ship – hence the name 'heads', which came into universal use for ships' toilets. They were set in such an exposed position that they could be kept clean by the action of the sea breaking over the bows – what they must have been like in a calm sea defies imagination.

Unicorn is still at the beginning of what will, no doubt, be a long process of restoration. When completed, she will be one of the finest of all our preserved craft, though a rival is taking shape further south on Teesside – a rival that represents the start of a new age of warships.

7   *Ironclad*

Necessity is said to be the mother of invention. If wars can be said to be necessary, then they provide conclusive proof of the truth of that statement. The war of 1812 is a case in point, for out of that war came many new ideas for warships, most of them originating in America. It was here that the first steam-powered battleship, the *Demologos*, was built, to a design by Robert Fulton. It was a remarkable craft, with the paddles set between twin hulls for protection. It was launched in 1814, but it never saw active service, and did not start a fashion for armed catamarans. Other more conventional paddle-steamers were built, the British finally joining in in 1821. Their scepticism over the value of the paddle-steamer in war is understandable. The paddles got in the way of the guns, machinery was heavy and took up too much space, coal consumption was enormous and the engines were set in the most vulnerable position, close to the water-line. The future of steam power looked more promising with the introduction of the screw-propeller in the 1830s. Francis Pettit Smith did much to promote its use in Britain, while its other inventor, John Ericsson, did the same in America.

New problems soon began to appear. A French artillery officer, Henry-Joseph Paixhams, persuaded French authorities that the future lay not in wooden walls lobbing cannon balls, but in steamers armed with guns firing shells horizontally. He gave a successful demonstration of his theory in 1824, when in one concentrated burst of firing he all but blew an old 80-gun ship of the line out of the water. The search was now on for a protection against these new weapons, and the first notion was to use iron instead of wood for the hull. Lairds of Birkenhead tried to persuade the Admiralty in London to order new battleships built of iron, but their Lordships declined the offer and Lairds had to be content with building two armed paddle-steamers for the East India Company in 1839 and an iron frigate for Mexico 10 years later. Small iron ships were ordered, but still the Admiralty refused to order iron battleships. Tests carried out in 1849 and 1850 showed that their lack of enthusiasm was justified. As the official report put it: 'The number and destructive nature of the splinters produced by the breaking up of the shot would cause a few well directed shot to clear away whole guns' crews.' Asking the men to shelter behind iron plate was like asking them to take cover behind a sheet of plate glass while someone threw stones at it.

There were more hopeful experiments in France in 1845. Dupuy de Lôme put forward a proposal for an iron steamer, reinforced by laminated iron armour, but there, as in Britain, opinion was moving away from the whole idea of iron warships. The Crimean War saw a modest success for floating iron batteries, but these were a long way from being warships. Then, in 1855, the French began a major shipbuilding programme, planning to construct 40 battleships, 20 frigates, 30 corvettes and 60 smaller vessels. They were all, without exception, to be built in wood. Eighteen months later, the French began to assess the

The submarine Alliance *on display, like an H.G.Wells spaceship*

power of the new rifled guns, and came to the conclusion that they would prove destructive if used against wooden ships. All work was stopped. What they now needed, they decided, was a fast, well-armed and well-armoured battleship of at least 4,000 tons displacement.

HMS Warrior, *1860*

The chances of acquiring such a ship increased in January 1857, when Dupuy de Lôme was appointed Directeur de Matériel, equivalent to the British Surveyor of the Navy. He had already shown himself a bold designer with his screw-steamer *Napoléon*, which could reach a speed of 14 knots. It was this design which was to form the basis for his most famous ship, the *Gloire*, launched in 1859. At 5,620 tons, it was 500 tons more than *Napoléon*, yet de Lôme achieved similar performance with similar engines by increasing the length rather than the beam. She was not the 'go anywhere, fight anywhere' warship of the traditional fleets, but was designed solely for use in European waters where coaling was not a problem. Sail was reduced to a minimum. She had armour-plating fastened on to her hull, 11 cms thick on the upper strakes, 12 cms thick on the lower. In her trials she reached a speed of 13 knots, and could stay at sea for 27 days cruising at 8 knots. She was a formidable ship, and de Lôme declared that one such vessel in a fleet of wooden walls would be like a lion in a flock of sheep.

The British responded at once. The initiative had come from France, but Britain was still the world's leading technological power. Her iron industry, in particular, was superior to that of France. When news of the *Gloire* came through, the Admiralty put out a simple design brief – build us, they said, a warship that can overtake and destroy any other warship on the water. Designers Sir Isaac Watts and John Scott Russell accepted the challenge, and the result was *Warrior*, laid down in 1859 and launched in 1861.

Technically, *Warrior* was a frigate, carrying all her armament on a single deck, but this was a frigate more than capable of holding her

Warrior *at Hartlepool*

The new bow shortly after fitting into place

place among the ships of the line. She was, without doubt, the most powerful warship afloat; faster, bigger, better armed and better protected than the *Gloire*. She was also the first of the new breed of warships. *Gloire* was, in effect, the old-style wooden wall, dressed up in a suit of armour: *Warrior* was an iron ship with additional armour-plating. She was powered by the latest thing in marine engines, the Penn Trunk engine. This had connecting rods attached directly to the pistons, eliminating the piston-rod and so saving space. They had a rating of 5,000-indicated horsepower and could drive *Warrior* through the water at a speed of over 14 knots – in spite of still working with steam at the very low pressure of 20 p.s.i. *Warrior* could cruise for 8 days at 11 knots, but to help her stay at sea and cruise in distant waters, she was fully rigged with sail on 3 masts, though they look very small for a 380-feet long iron ship. With all sails and stunsails set she logged up a speed of 13 knots, and with steam and sail working together she recorded a speed of 17.5 knots on a run from Portsmouth to Plymouth in 1861.

The first stage of restoration includes removing the junk accumulated over the years

Everything about *Warrior* was the latest and best that industry could devise. Instead of the old muzzle-loading guns, she was supplied with the new breech-loaders. In fact, breech-loaders were in short supply, so when fitted out beside her ten new 110-pounders and four 70-pounders, she also had twenty-six of the old-style muzzle-loading 68-pounders, though these had been greatly improved by rifling the barrels, which gave a much more accurate trajectory to the shell. To the great consternation and dismay of the assembled ordnance officers, it was found on trials that the 'improved' 110-pounders were less effective than the old-fashioned smaller guns. So, in 1867, breech-loaders went out and muzzle-loaders came in – and it was to be some time before the problem of building an efficient breech-loader was to be solved. Nevertheless, *Warrior* was still the mightiest ship afloat, the first of a new generation of ironclads. She was not, perhaps, as impregnable as her designers believed, but that was never put to the test. She never went to war, and was eventually relegated to duty as a pontoon at Pembroke Docks, machinery and masts gone, her decks encased in concrete. In 1979 she was rescued by the Maritime Trust who arranged for her to be towed to Hartlepool for restoration. There she lies, no more than a hull at the time of writing, but a hugely impressive one.

Warrior represents a quite different design principle from that used in *Victory*. One is struck not so much by the change in size as by the change in proportion. Both vessels have approximately the same beam, but *Warrior* is twice as long: it would be unfair to say that one is a carthorse to the other's racehorse, but that is undeniably the impression they create. Differences in scale become even more apparent inside the vessel, and it is here, too, that the really distinguishing feature of the new vessel can be seen. Walking along the gun deck, one can almost believe oneself back in the man-of-war, with the gun ports punctuating the sides. But walk up to those gun ports and inspect them more closely and the differences at once become apparent. The hull is enormously thick, and you can see that it is made up of a kind of sandwich. On the inside is the iron hull of the ship, then a backing of teak, 18 inches thick, and beyond that $4\frac{1}{2}$-inch-thick wrought-iron plate. It was this combination of wood and iron that overcame the problem of splintering, enabling the builders to combine the virtues of the iron hull and armour-plating. Yet the armour is not continuous. The plating extends 16 feet above the water-line and 6 feet below and for 213 feet of the length, leaving 83 feet at either end as unprotected metal. What the effect of a hit in this region would have been was never discovered – and perhaps it is just as well. The risks were minimised to some extent in the hull, which was divided up into a series of water-tight compartments, something which had never been possible in the old wooden boats.

Warrior is a curious amalgam of the old and the new. With her fine lines, powerful engine, iron hull and armour-plating she looked to-

The gun deck of Warrior, *similar in many respects to* Victory *and* Unicorn

A boarded-up gun port, showing Warrior's *unique construction: an iron hull, backed by wood, the outside covered in armour plating*

wards the future, and in terms of sheer increase in size she represents a bigger step forward along that particular road than the navy had made in the past three centuries of its existence. Yet in other ways, she reflects the thinking of the past. As well as being a steamer, she is also a fully-rigged three-masted sailing ship, and her armament is deployed just as on *Victory*: rows of guns lined up ready to deliver a broadside. Yet she remains a remarkable craft, at once both the first and last of her line: Britain's first battleship in the modern sense of the word and, amazingly, her last, for no other has survived. Innovation continued, however, long after *Warrior* was launched.

The next major changes came with advances in gunnery – the end of the age of the broadside and the beginning of the age of the turret gun. As with the screw-propeller, there were two inventors with claims to be first with the new idea, and again John Ericsson was one of the claimants. It was certainly Ericsson who was the first to see his idea put into practice and tried in war. Ericsson appreciated that warfare was coming to depend more and more on the technological expertise of the combatants. As the American Civil War began, he wrote to Lincoln: 'The time has come Mr. President, when our cause will have to be sustained not by numbers, but by superior weapons . . . it is susceptible of demonstration that, if you can apply our mechanical resources to the fullest extent, you can destroy the enemy without enlisting another man.'

Ericsson designed the *Monitor*, an iron vessel with such an incredibly low free-board that even the lightest of swells set the decks awash. On top of this was perched the circular gun turret. The whole thing looked, declared a contemporary, like a cheese-box on a raft. In 1862 *Monitor* went into battle against the Confederate wooden wall, the *Merrimack*. They battered away at each other at long range for 6 hours, neither doing any real harm. *Monitor*'s 11-inch guns lacked the necessary power, while the shot from *Merrimack* bounced off *Monitor* like hailstones off a tin roof – and did about as much damage. The encounter at least demonstrated that the turret was less vulnerable to attack than the old gun ports.

In Britain, Captain Cowper Coles was an enthusiastic advocate of what he called the cupola turret. It was tested on an old floating battery and was bombarded by both cannon and rifled guns, and even after 33 direct hits had been recorded, the turret still worked. The cupola turret was deemed a success, and a new 3,880-ton warship, the *Prince Albert*, was commissioned in 1862, carrying four 9-inch guns in individual turrets. They were cumbersome devices, which had to be moved round by a crew of 18 men using hand-spikes and a simple ratchet mechanism out on the deck. As the crew were outside the turret and the gunnery officer inside and communication between the two was somewhat difficult, gun-laying tended to be a hit-and-miss affair, with rather more emphasis on the latter. The *Prince Albert* had, however, established a precedent. The multi-turreted warship had arrived.

The warships that fought the great naval engagements of the Second World War built on the foundations laid down in the previous century. They were big, armoured steamships armed with guns in rotating turrets, natural successors to *Warrior* and *Prince Albert*, though they neither looked nor performed like them. If there was one factor which separated them most clearly from their predecessors, it was the great range and accuracy of their guns, and great range had many implications for battles at sea and for the way ships were designed. This is well exemplified in the cruiser *HMS Belfast*, now permanently moored as a floating museum in London.

Belfast is moored on the south bank of the Thames above Tower Bridge. The best way to appreciate her size is to approach on foot from the direction of London Bridge Station. Walking parallel to the river, you look along a side street and see the bows, walk down to the next corner and see the bridge, and so on, street by street until you reach the stern. Seen from the opposite bank, she seems slightly less impressive, in the wide reaches of the river, than when glimpsed, a bit at a time.

The warships of the Second World War were perhaps the last we shall ever see in which sheer size mattered. We are now in the age of missiles and nuclear warheads, when the smallest vessels are capable of spreading unbelievable destruction. But in those days, fire power depended on size. *Belfast* herself was not even a battleship but a cruiser, though at 11,550 tons she was a formidable fighting ship. The bare statistics alone give good indication of how far ship design had advanced since the previous century: length overall, 613 feet, beam 66 feet, maximum speed, 32 knots, range, travelling at the cruising speed of 13 knots, 7,000 miles. The hull is steel, the power comes from oil-fired turbines.

Warships are built to engage in warfare: speed, manœuvrability and range are there at the service of the guns. And the changes in the armament are at least as dramatic as the others. It is a mark of progress of a sort, a measure of the accelerating pace of technological change,

Left. HMS Belfast *on the*
Thames at London

Right. *The engine-room which*
houses the steam turbines

that while the sailors of Nelson's navy would have been impressed by the guns of *Warrior*, the men from *Warrior* would have been astonished by *Belfast*. They would have recognised that they were in a new age of naval warfare.

The main armament consists of twelve 6-inch guns, carried on 4 turrets, 2 forward and 2 aft. There is great flexibility here, for the guns have elevations up to 45° and a training arc of 120° on either side of the fore and aft line. Until the turret came into use, it was necessary to bring the whole ship round to get the guns lined up for a broadside, but now it is the guns that can be moved – and moved rapidly. They can be brought round at 5° a second, and once in position they can fire 8 rounds a minute. It was not just this new-found flexibility that had brought change to naval gunnery – the range of the guns had also increased enormously. They could send a 112-pound shell just over 14 miles so that, in the unlikely eventuality of someone bringing them back into use, the commuters on Surbiton station could find themselves under fire from guns at Tower Bridge.

Fourteen miles is a long way – certainly further than one can see from *Belfast* today, though here visibility is largely limited by surrounding buildings, not a problem at sea. But even if one could see the target that far away, it would require something rather more sophisticated than the keen eye of a gunner to hit it at that range. The gunner needs to know how far away the enemy is and in what direction, and if the enemy is another ship, he also needs to know in what direction it is moving and how fast in relation to his own course and speed. And at extreme range calculations are critical, for a 1-degree error in arc would put the shell a quarter of a mile from its target.

HMS Belfast is in every way a fascinating ship. It is a completely self-contained unit: on board is everything the crew of over 600 might need, from baker to dentist. There is a hospital to keep the crew fit, and a full-scale engineering workshop to keep the engine turning. And splendid engines they are, a connection back to Turbinia, for *Belfast* was supplied with Parsons' geared turbines, arranged in 4 units, each with a high- and low-pressure turbine working in series, supplied with superheated steam at 300 p.s.i. Impressive as it all is, it means very little unless the shells leaving the gun will eventually hit their target. The first essential is to locate the enemy.

When *Belfast* was commissioned in 1939, just one month before the outbreak of war, she carried two Walrus amphibious aircraft, which acted as her eyes. In her first success, that was all she needed, for on 9 October she intercepted the German liner *Cap Norte*, boarded her and took her captive. It was her first success of the war – and nearly her last. Next month, steaming out of the Forth of Firth, she encountered the new German weapon, the magnetic mine, and was nearly lost. The damage was immense and *Belfast* was out of action for nearly three years. When she came back, she had been given new and better eyes – radar. Radar brought new accuracy to the hunt for enemy vessels and to the direction of the six-inch guns, and interpreting and using the information from the new invention called for a complex control system within the ship.

In the days when the Walrus flew off the deck – a period which lasted until June 1943 – it was planes that were expected to provide the first contact with the enemy. At a later date, first indications came through radar, and all information on movement round the *Belfast* – in the air, on the surface or under the waves – was fed to the operations room immediately below the navigation bridge. Surface craft and submarines were plotted in one section, aircraft in another. The Gun Direction Room helped with the selection of targets for engagement. If a target was in visual range, then the directions would be given from the gun direction platform over the bridge. Once the captain had given the order to the 6-inch gun director to 'acquire and engage' the target, then everything became centred on a tiny space, under the water-line and protected by armour-plating – the six-inch transmitting station.

At the centre of the transmitting station is the Admiralty Fire Control Table. This is, in effect, a complex mechanical computer, into which all relevant information is fed – own ship's speed and course, enemy's speed and direction and course, range to the target and, where appropriate, height of the target. As any or all of these factors could be changing all the time, the calculator was an essential piece of equipment. It took all these factors into account and reduced them down to the necessary figures for gun elevation and training. The

The navigation bridge, control centre for the whole ship

The operations room on Belfast. The charts are laid out to show the Battle of North Cape

turrets were swung round to the correct angle, individual guns elevated as instructed. Approval to fire the guns came from the captain, and actual firing was controlled from two Director Control Towers, one forward and one aft. Guns were brought to the ready by an order which seems to take us back two centuries – 'Broadsides'.

The gun-layers received the basic information from the transmitting station and as soon as the pointers were lined up, the 'gun ready' lamps came on, the director squeezed the trigger. The broadside fired, and a spotting display showed a radar picture of the target area, indicating just where the shots landed. Corrections could be instantaneously made and the guns were prepared for the next salvo.

The six-inch transmitting station, showing the fire control table, used for gunnery calculations

Preparing the guns was the work of a well-organised and highly efficient team of 46 men to a turret. Each turret had a turret captain, a sight-layer, a turret trainer, sight-setter and telephone operator and 7 men to each gun. The guns were kept supplied through a hoist system, linking up with the magazines below decks, and the other 20 men worked down there, supplying the explosive charges, cordite and shells. Once a gun was fired, it was lowered for reloading, then packed with a shell, a 30-pound load of cordite in a silk bag – silk because it burns without trace – and a tube of high explosive which was ignited by an electric spark. This, in turn, fired the cordite which sent the shell on its way. Here, too, there is a reminder of naval warfare a century and more ago, for the shell is rammed home with a rammer exactly like that used on *Victory*, with a sponge at the end for cleaning the breech after firing.

This whole business of arming and firing *Belfast*'s guns takes a good deal longer to describe than it took to perform. That the system and the crew that applied it were efficient is clear from *Belfast*'s long and distinguished record. Perhaps the most famous battle in which she was involved and the one which most clearly demonstrates the virtues

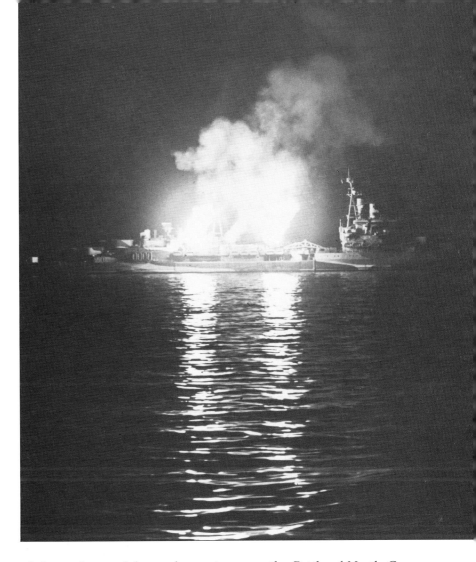

HMS Belfast *firing on the Normandy shore in June 1944*

of the cruiser and her radar system was the Battle of North Cape, which ended in the sinking of the German battle-cruiser *Scharnhorst* in December 1943. The complex manœuvres of pursued and pursuers are laid out, as they were plotted, in *Belfast*'s control room. Vice Admiral Burnett in *Belfast* was able to follow his prey on the radar through the dark of the Arctic night as the *Scharnhorst* squirmed across the ocean in a desperate bid to elude her pursuers. Without the new eyes of the navy, she would certainly have got away. This was by no means the only, nor the last, great action in which *Belfast* was involved. She worked with the Russian convoys, led the cruiser bombardment of the Normandy coast on D-Day, and later took part in the Korean War.

We have concentrated on only one aspect of the *Belfast* story – her big guns. There was more to the vessel than that, nor was that her only armament, for she carried twelve 4-inch guns and a battery of anti-aircraft weapons. She also carried torpedoes, weapons more closely associated with the vessel that was destined to gain ever increasing importance in twentieth-century warfare – the submarine.

The submarine has a surprisingly long history. A submarine of sorts was demonstrated on the Thames as early as 1620, which worked on the principle of filling a converted boat with ballast until it was on the point of sinking and then rowing it along so that it barely showed above water. The only result was total exhaustion of the crew. The Americans were the first to achieve success, through Robert Fulton of steamboat fame and David Bushnell. The latter's *Turtle* was actually used by the Americans against the British fleet in 1776. It was an egg-shaped device, which was submerged by flooding tanks with sea water, and which moved through the water by means of hand-operated propellers. The idea was that it should dive under the enemy's hull, at which point a gunpowder charge with a clockwork fuse would be attached to the ship's bottom. It was sent into action against *HMS Eagle*, but as the Americans had not heard about the copper sheathing on the bottom of the hull they failed to puncture the metal. Though the mission failed, the submarine, at least, had worked.

Fulton's invention, which more closely resembled a modern submarine, was tried out in France, where the inventor gave a convincing demonstration of its use by attaching a charge to a floating hull and blowing it up. The French were reluctant to use so fearful a weapon

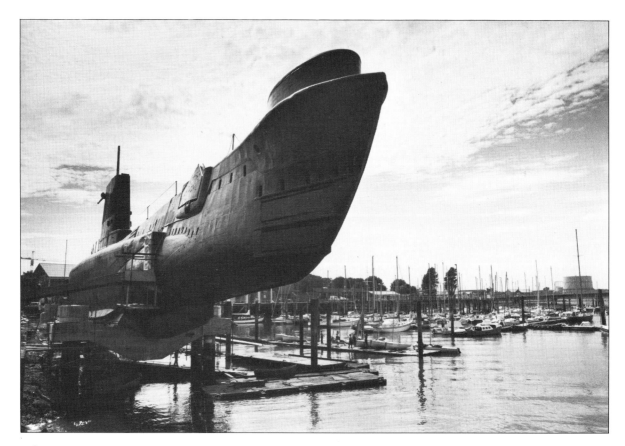

and the inventor went off to hawk his wares to the enemy. The British were equally displeased by his work. He was too successful. Naval officers preferred the *status quo*, potting at each other with broadsides rather than skulking beneath the waves.

The next advances in design were the work of a Bavarian soldier, Wilhelm Bauer, who used moveable weights to enable his vessel to dive at an angle. The trouble was that though the craft worked, it still had no suitable weapon. The answer was the torpedo, which started out as an explosive charge fixed on the end of a pole attached to a small craft, which then charged at the enemy like a jousting knight with his lance. These spar torpedoes came in during the American Civil War and were used by the Confederates. The tiny craft were known as 'Davids', though whether they were liable to do more damage to themselves than to the opposing Goliaths was a matter of conjecture. In April 1864, a 9-man crew took their David to attack the warship *Housatonic*. The warship was sunk, but her little attacker went down with her. Nevertheless, it seemed clear that a new and potent weapon had arrived. All the major navies at once began work on submarines,

Left. HMS Alliance *raised out of the water and ready for the public*

Right. *The torpedo tubes*

except the British, who still regarded the whole thing as somehow unsporting, and only started research of their own in 1901 when it was clear they had no choice.

The diesel engines for surface running

The effectiveness of submarines, not only against military targets but also against merchant shipping, was amply demonstrated in the two world wars. By then, the submarine had acquired its main characteristics, through development in a number of countries. From America came the idea of hydroplanes attached to the hull which could keep the vessel on an even keel without constant adjustments of the ballast. From France and Spain came the idea of the electric motor for underwater travel. The French again provided the solution to the problem of running on the surface, when they brought in the diesel engine to replace the dangerous petrol engine.

A British engineer, Robert Whitehead, working in Fiume in what is now Yugoslavia, added a final, vital ingredient. He provided the weapon – the self-propelling torpedo. Now the submarine could attack from a distance, but at the beginning of the century few people realised just how devastating a weapon this was. The lesson was learned in the First World War. In 1914, Germany had 29 submarines in service: by 1918 390 had been built and between them they had sunk over 6,000 ships, a total tonnage of 11 million. The submarine had been thought of at the beginning of the war as a kind of underwater warship, ready to engage in battle with other warships. A new and more deadly role was soon found, as a hunter of merchant ships. When, in the past, merchant ships had been attacked, they had been taken as prizes: the submarine sank them instead and nearly won a greater prize for Germany. The devastation of the British merchant fleet almost turned the fortune of war.

The submarine war of 1939–45 was fought as fiercely as that of the earlier war. Britain was always the more susceptible to submarine attack, because as an island nation she needed to make far greater use of sea-borne trade than did Germany. Nevertheless, the British, too, built submarines and one of these has been preserved as an adjunct to the Submarine Museum at the naval base, *HMS Dolphin*, where submariners still train. *Alliance* is an A-class, the largest the British built during the war, with a dead weight of 1,150 tons. She was completed in 1945, just in time to miss active service, but she was fully fitted out for war, so that the visitor has a remarkably vivid picture of what life was like for the submariner.

Seen from the outside, *Alliance* has that sinister air common to all submarines: partly it is the unrelieved black of the hull, partly it is the shape, so strongly reminiscent of the ocean's predators. Perched on top is the fin, a streamlined casing surrounding the periscopes and the conning tower. Clambering down through the hatchway, it is hard to escape a sensation of instant claustrophobia. The hull may look quite large from the outside, but in fact the bottom two-thirds is taken up

Electric motors for submerged running

Even the heads are complicated on a submarine

with tanks, and only the top third is available for the crew of 68 ratings and 6 officers. They share the space with a mass of machinery, and given that *Alliance* is only 285 feet long by 22 feet beam, everything clearly has to be packed very close indeed.

Forward and aft are the torpedo compartments. The torpedoes themselves are loaded into the tubes by sliding down rails on a trolley, before being hoisted into place by block and tackle. Engines take up a good deal of the rest of the room. The diesels are Vickers straight eights, each of 2,500 horsepower. Using her diesels she can make 20 knots on the surface, but when partly submerged and snorkling, with only the tip of the fin above water, she used one engine for power and the other for recharging her batteries. When wholly submerged, she could work down to a depth of 650 feet, and only the electric motor was used, together with the burners that got rid of the hydrogen from the batteries. As with *Belfast*, space is taken up with navigation and control rooms, made yet more complex in the submarine by movement not just through two but through three dimensions. The objective, however, remains the same: to hunt and destroy.

Submarines are a self-contained world. This is true of all ships that have to go on long tours of duty, but it has a special significance in the submarine. It is often said that submariners feel that they have more in common with other submariners, even those fighting on the opposite side, than they do with sailors who man surface ships. It is easy to see why. Conditions are quite unlike those in other vessels. Space is so limited that the crew work on a 'hot bunk' system – as one rating got back from his watch, he had to turf out his successor and climb into his bunk. The stoker's mess occupies a space no larger than 12 feet by 8. Here a dozen men slept in 3 tiers of bunks, and here they took whatever leisure time was available. For most of us, who have never served in a submarine, it is the sensation of being closed in that makes the vessel so special, and it would be a very unimaginative visitor who did not think for a moment of what it means to have to escape from a stricken submarine. The crew had to sit and wait, breathing through air tubes while the water built up inside. Finally, when pressure was equalised, the hatch would fly open and the submariners shot up to the surface.

There were, of course, happier aspects of submarine life – and the submariner always had one never-fail joke to play on any unpopular 'rider', as visitors are known. Because of the pressure differences between the outside and the inside of the vessel, toilets can only be emptied by using a complex system of valves. Anyone using them in the wrong sequence got his own back – literally. This will not, however, apply to *Alliance*'s visitors as they make their way down the length of the hull. One thing they are all going to want to do is to peer through the periscope. As they swing it round for a view across the bay they come to *Victory*, and we too have come full circle in this brief look at preserved naval craft.

8   *Home from the Sea*

Ships and men need a home to return to: a harbour where the ship can be anchored, moored or beached in safety, where essential repairs can be carried out, stores replenished, cargo loaded and unloaded, where men can take a rest from the sea, where old crews can be discharged and new recruited. The word 'harbour' tends to conjure up a picture of a man-made complex, but this need not be the case. Any spot with deep enough water, that is sheltered from the weather, can be a harbour, and most of the great harbours of the world began as purely natural features which happened to meet those requirements, and which man later improved.

This improvement of the natural harbour goes right back into the ancient world. Massive harbour works were carried out in the Mediterranean at least as far back as the time of the Phoenicians, though most traces have long since disappeared, if not under modern works, then under the additions of those indefatigable builders, the Romans. Britain cannot boast any ancient harbour works to match such magnificent remains as those of Leptis Magna in North Africa. However, spread around the coastline are examples of almost every conceivable type of harbour, so that it is not difficult to get an idea of the way in which harbours developed, and the effect of those developments on the vessels that used them.

A good place to start is Cornwall, for not only does it have the longest coastline of any English county, but it also contains a rich variety of harbours, serving a variety of users. Most people will think first of the 'picturesque' fishing ports – a description which was rarely used a century ago. Murray's *Handbook for Travellers in Devon and Cornwall* of 1850 speaks instead of 'those antiquated fishing towns which are viewed more agreeably from a distance'. Antiquated, in the sense of long established, many of them certainly are, and in the majority of cases one can see exactly how they developed out of natural features. A river estuary, or a quiet bay protected by cliffs and headland, was the starting point for most, places where boats could be safely run up on the beach and as safely launched again into the waves. One could name a dozen spots where geography has determined the site for a little village and harbour.

Improvement of the natural site often dates back a long way. Mousehole was described as a port in the early thirteenth century, and the harbour was improved in the 1930s, when a quay was built to provide added protection. The harbour wall is a feature of many of the small ports – for example, Polperro, Port Isaac and Mevagissey. There were frequent alterations, some made because better facilities were required, some forced by circumstances. At Mevagissey a fine new harbour was built between 1888 and 1890 to replace the works of the previous century, but it was demolished in the great gales of March 1891, and had to be completely rebuilt.

Albert Dock, Liverpool

165

The fishing harbour under the sheltering cliffs: Crail in Fife

The commonest form developed was that in which two walls were built out from the shore, curling round towards each other like a pair of claws, leaving a narrow entrance through which boats could pass into calm waters. The design of breakwaters to take account of tides and prevailing winds was much improved in the eighteenth century, when engineers like John Smeaton put harbour design on to something like a scientific footing. The two quays which enclose the outer harbour at Charlestown, for example, have quite different shapes, each shape suiting the situation of that quay. Their names, banjo quay and knuckle quay, accurately describe their shapes. The fishing harbours offer many variations on the basic theme of enclosing breakwaters.

An alternative to the construction of expensive stonework is to move the harbour further down a navigable river, which will automatically provide protection against the worst of the coastal storms. And the further inland it is, the more protected it will be. This is not a particularly appealing prospect for fishermen who want the shortest journey to the fishing ground and the quickest route home with the catch. It is very appealing, however, to those whose business lies in trade and the carriage of cargoes. This was especially true in the days before the major road improvements of the late eighteenth and early nineteenth centuries, when land transport was notoriously bad. There was a good deal to be said in favour of bringing cargo as far inland as possible by water. Building work could often be reduced to a minimum for these river ports. All that was needed to offer a functional port was a solid quay to which a vessel could be moored for loading and unloading, a crane to help with the work, and a warehouse for storage.

The quay at Cotehele, with the Tamar barge Shamrock

Cotehele, on the Cornish bank of the Tamar, meets all those requirements, and one can see ample evidence of the likely cargoes in the lime kilns that surround the quay. Along the river bank, especially as one moves upstream, is evidence of even greater activity in the ruined chimneys and engine-houses that mark the once famous tin and copper mines. And, indeed, as one gets to the heart of the tin-mining area, there is evidence of other, far busier ports in the once important shipbuilding centre of Calstock and the even larger port of Morwellham, which served the mighty Devon Great Consols Mine.

It is hard, now, to appreciate just how busy this area once was. It seems an unlikely major trading route, for the river has extravagant bends and a narrow deep-water channel. Like all ports set a long way up river, those of the Tamar could only take vessels up to a certain size – and the limitations were increased when no major dredging work was put in hand to make deep-water docks. The little quay at Cotehele was certainly not capable of accommodating big ships, even if they could have negotiated the winding river. It could, however, take the smaller vessels, which could either make short runs around the coast or carry cargoes on to the bigger, deep-sea ships. One of these has been restored and given a permanent berth beside the quay at Cotehele – the Tamar barge, *Shamrock*.

Shamrock is a ketch-rigged sailing barge, which is to say that she is fore- and aft-rigged on two masts. She has gaffsails on mainmast and mizzen and two jibsails. She was built in 1899 at Devonport for the somewhat unromantic trade of carrying animal manure from Torpoint on the west bank of the Tamar to Plymouth. She is not a large vessel, only 57 feet 6 inches long, with shallow draught but very wide in the beam. When grounded she would stay upright, and carts could be brought up on either side so that the manure could be shovelled straight into the hold. The shallow draught made her ideal for the job, but did not provide the stability that was needed if she was to make coastal journeys. There was nothing to 'bite' on the water. The builders solved that problem by adding a centre board, a shaped timber which could be lowered through the floor, acting as a keel and performing the same function as the lee-boards on the Thames barges.

In 1919, *Shamrock* was sold and converted into a thorough seagoing vessel, when a new deep false keel was added. Hatch coamings were raised, a bowsprit added and an auxiliary engine put in. In her new guise she was used to carry stone from quarries on the River Lynher round the coast as far as Falmouth. From the 30s to the 50s, she worked out of Truro carrying road-stone and then passed to a salvage company. In 1974, she was acquired by the National Trust, who also own Cotehele Quay. They went to the National Maritime Museum for expert help with the job of restoration.

Shamrock at anchor

Shamrock was in a wretched condition: her timbers rotted, rigging and
sails gone. It was not so much a restoration job as a complete rebuild,
and that is just what she had, with no effort spared to return her to the
condition she was in during the 1920s, during her days of coastal and
river trading. Appropriate fittings such as blocks and cleats were
hunted down in neighbouring shipyards. Rigging was specially made
by the National Maritime Museum at Cotehele Mill out of manila rope,
and traditional canvas sails were made by the Falmouth sail-makers
who had made her last working mainsail. Framing and planking,
masts and spars were all replaced and she now has a connection with
another West Country boat, for her bowsprit originally belonged to the
Kathleen and May.

The scene at Cotehele is one that had its equivalent along all the
major rivers of Britain. The quay itself is simple, constructed from local
stone, with stone bollards lining the edge. A single hand crane was all
it could boast in terms of mechanical aids. The warehouse is stone-
built, with loading bays facing the water, and now houses a museum,
where exhibits tell the story of the Tamar when it was a bustling,
thriving highway. Today a few small craft and pleasure boats pass
along the river, but in the summer of 1981 there was a true memory of
older times, when *Shamrock* took again to the water.

Cotehele represents a small, riverside development, but until
quite recently even such major docks as those of the Port of London
offered little more than we can see here. The differences were not
differences of kind but of scale. There was the same system of quays
built into the river bank, backed by warehouses, and large vessels
either came alongside the quays at high tide or rode in the tideway to
be loaded and unloaded by lighters. Many such ports were over-
whelmed by later developments, but a few, often because their trade
simply died away, became, as it were, fossilised, stuck at one particular point in their history. Just such a port complex – an expanded
Cotehele – can be seen on the River Lune at Lancaster.

Lancaster had been a port, but in a small way, since at least the
thirteenth century. In the middle of the eighteenth century, local
merchants and shipowners managed to get an Act through Parliament
authorising the establishment of a Port Commission, and work could
begin on dredging and improving the navigation of the Lune. There
followed a busy period of building wharves and warehouses to handle
the increased trade. There was hardwood from America to feed the
recently established furniture works of Robert Gillow. There was sugar
and rum from the West Indies and it was on the Lune, at Sunderland
Point, that the first bales of cotton were landed from the New World.
Add to that a flourishing coastal trade, and you have the makings of a
successful port. The new waterfront complex was named St George's
Quay, and was soon lined with warehouses, their gable ends facing
the water.

The eighteenth-century warehouses come in various sizes, but tend to follow the same general pattern. They are multi-storeyed stone buildings, with many windows and rows of loading bays, topped by simple hoists. Some of the hoists are quite sophisticated metal devices, others are little more than crudely-shaped timbers. So too with the buildings, some of which are quite grand, with beautifully dressed stone façades, while others have the jig-saw look that comes from building in random rubble, where unevenly shaped blocks are all fitted together to make up the wall. In between the warehouses are the houses and offices of the merchants, having to squeeze into whatever space was left over by their bigger commercial neighbours. And lauding it over them all is the Customs House, designed by Richard Gillow, son of the furniture manufacturer, and completed in 1765. It still looks handsome, with its fine Palladian portico, but HM Customs have long gone, leaving their building to serve as an electricity sub-station.

The Lune at Lancaster

Lancaster's new port was begun with great enthusiasm in the 1750s – a century later and it was all but dead. The navigation was further improved in the 1840s and new warehouses were built downstream from St George's Quay, but Lancashire had changed. The major industry was cotton, and its centre was further south. Lancaster could take vessels of around 200 tons, but that was not enough for the new industry. Lancaster and the Lune simply could not compete with Liverpool and the Mersey.

Right. *The handsome Customs House*

Below. *Crude wooden hoist on a Lancaster warehouse*

Liverpool has as ancient a history as Lancaster, having been given borough status by King John in 1207, but its importance as a major port only began to emerge in the eighteenth century. At first sight, it must have seemed an unlikely location for a dock development, on a windswept estuary with fast tides swirling between sandbanks and shallows. The Pool itself was a big curved inlet, a major feature of the river until the beginning of the eighteenth century. It was there that the first Liverpool dock, and the first commercial dock in Britain, was built. A London engineer, Thomas Steers, devised the plan for enclosing the Pool water behind a sea wall, to create a closed dock of some 3½ acres which could provide shelter for a whole fleet of ships.

This was a wet dock, one in which deep water could be retained at all states of the tide, and it became the focal point for new development in Liverpool so that, in time, it was surrounded by buildings and streets, while the dock itself was so full of boats that it was difficult to see where town ended and dock began. It was joined to the river by a small channel which frequently became clogged with boats. To relieve the congestion, a new dock was built and the tidal basin was closed off

The gateman's hut by the ruined lock gates that link the Liverpool dock complex to the Mersey

by lock-gates, so that it, too, became a wet dock. This area was to see many more changes over the years, but it was the nucleus from which the entire Liverpool dock complex developed. It is now, appropriately, also the site of Liverpool's new maritime museum.

The museum is still at the very beginning of its development, which means that although there are exciting changes in the offing, the dock scheme and layout remain relatively uncluttered. Starting by the river, there is the Canning Half-Tide Dock, joined directly to the river by lock-gates. It is known as a half-tide dock because, unlike the wet docks beyond it, it cannot be used at all states of the tide, but only when the water level is high enough in the river. We can see the truly massive stonework that pushed the dock area out into the river, for, where most docks are excavated out of the land and then filled with water, the first Liverpool docks were made by enclosing the old Pool. Here, too, are the pilotage buildings of 1883, home of the pilots who steered the big ships through the complex channels of the Mersey.

Next to the Half-Tide Dock are two graving docks, into which vessels needing work to the hull could be floated. Earlier, work to the

The graving dock, Liverpool Maritime Museum

Superb masonry is a feature of the dock construction

Below. *Canning Dock at the end of the last century, with the Customs House, now demolished*

hull had involved careening a vessel, pulling it over on its side until it was almost horizontal. In this case the water was gradually drained out of the dock, leaving the ship literally high and dry, ready for the workmen. Around the dock can be seen some of the machines that made cargo handling somewhat easier in the twentieth century than it had ever been before: steam-cranes and even a steam-lorry, which replaced the old horse and waggon. The dock also contains a reminder of the days when it was used mainly by wooden ships, in the shape of the little boiler where pitch was heated up for sealing a ship's seams. An idea of the size of ship using the dock can be had from the huge iron bollards all round it.

Beyond the graving docks are the two old docks – the Canning Dock and the Salthouse Dock. Parts have gone, long since filled in, but one can still imagine the scenes of the last century, when these docks pierced right into the heart of the city. Here is an account of those times from a contemporary traveller, Richard Ayton, who took a trip round the British coast in 1814:

We had the luck to be present when two hundred sail, principally West Indiamen, were undocked in a single tide, and they made their way amidst such a confusion of obstacles, such a conflict of commands and opinions, such peals of swearing, such showers of blocks, snapping of rope, and cracking of bowsprits and quarter-boards, that it was really astonishing to us, to see them, all in the course of an hour, all safe and afloat in the river.

Now that the industrial revolution was turning Lancashire into the maufacturing capital of the world, the docks were simply not keeping pace. New development was needed, and it came about largely thanks to the work of one man, Jesse Hartley. He was appointed Civil Engineer and Superintendent of the Concerns of the Dock Estate of Liverpool in 1824 and stayed there until his death in 1860. During that time, he gave Liverpool 140 acres of wet dock and added almost 10 miles of quay. He also introduced whole new concepts into dock design at Liverpool.

The old docks had been unenclosed, open to the streets, and pilfering and theft had become diseases of epidemic proportions. Hartley's answer was to enclose all the new dockland within a boundary wall like the side of a fortress. The idea of surrounding a dock by warehouses and walls to create an enclosed space was not new – it had been pioneered in London, notably in St Katharine's Dock, the work of the architect Philip Hardwick and the civil engineer, Thomas Telford. Hartley developed the London ideas for his own greatest work, the Albert Dock, and because he was an essentially modest man, he had no hesitation whatsover in writing to Hardwick to ask for his comments on the scheme. It was to become, in fact, not only Hartley's masterwork but the grandest piece of dock development in the whole of Victorian Britain.

The steam lorry, one of the working survivors of dockside machinery at the museum, with Albert Dock behind

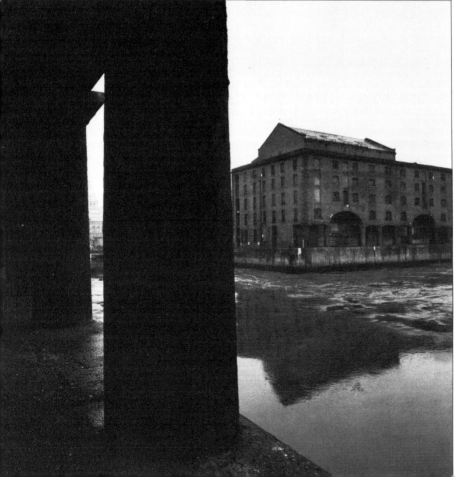

Left. *Colonnades look out over a sea of mud*

Albert Dock in the 1920s

Albert Dock lies next to the Canning Half-Tide Dock, and even now when its great basin is no more than a sea of mud and silt, it remains a uniquely impressive industrial monument – and one full of innovations. Hartley borrowed the basic notion from St Katharine's of building his warehouses right up to the quay edge, with the upper storeys carried out over the quay on colonnades. This had the great advantage that instead of having to unload from ship to quay and from quay to warehouse, goods could be taken straight from ship to warehouse. Cranes were built into the arches of the colonnades to make the process even simpler, lifts and hoists being powered hydraulically.

The principle of hydraulic power is simple. As water is pumped into a tall tower, known as an accumulator, the weight of the column of water provides a pressure that can then be used to drive machinery through a weighted ram in the accumulator tower. Water can be pumped up outside normal working hours, storing power for use later – rather in the way that a room storage-heater uses off-peak electricity. A hydraulic pumping station can be seen between the Half-Tide Dock and the Albert Dock warehouses.

These warehouses are themselves of very considerable interest. The ones at Lancaster are of stone, with wooden beams and joists, presenting a considerable fire hazard. Here the only materials used are stone, brick and iron. Brick arches spring from iron columns for the main support, but to see the most unusual feature of all you have to go up to the very top of the warehouses, 66 feet above the quay. The roof is undulating, an immense curved skin stretched over the building, made up of galvanised iron plates riveted together. And iron turns up again in unlikely circumstances in the dock offices, which are embellished with a classical portico, entirely constructed out of cast iron. Yet in spite of all the technical innovations it is the sheer size of the enterprise that still astonishes us today. A few simple statistics give some idea of the scale of the undertaking. Because it was built partly on quicksand, timber piles had to be driven in to form a solid base for building – almost 14,000 of them which, according to contemporary calculations, would – if laid end to end – stretch for 48 miles. The dock itself is 40 feet deep, and the warehouses cover a surface area of nearly 200,000 square feet. After that it is not surprising to learn that the whole scheme cost just over half a million pounds in the 1840s.

After Hartley's death, Liverpool docks continued to grow as a linear development along the riverside. Eventually they stretched for 7 miles, but now fortunes have declined. The ocean-going liners have disappeared; containerisation calls for quite different types of port facilities from those provided by the Victorians; the new generation of bulk carriers, such as the supertankers, are quite simply too large for the Mersey. So, the pattern has changed. In its day, Liverpool ousted Bristol from its pre-eminence on the west coast, and now it is Liverpool's turn to go into decline, just as London has had to do. Nevertheless, it was through the ever-growing port of Liverpool that the trade of the industrial revolution was carried.

The steam tug Portwey

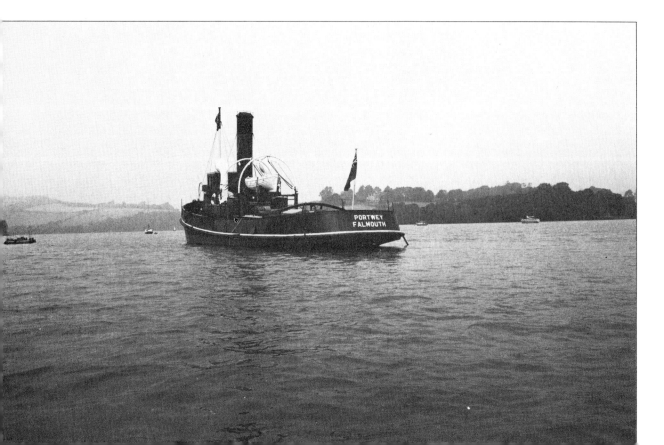

The changes that can be traced at Liverpool represented more than just an increase in scale over what had gone before; they showed the gradual implementation of a whole new way of thinking about docks. They also presented new problems in ship handling. Like the docks, the ships were getting bigger, and slotting them into their berths required the help of several, small, powerful but highly manœuvrable craft. If one had to select one vessel to epitomise the busy harbour scene in the early years of this century, it would have to be the steam tug. The tug needed to have the strength to move vessels many times its own size, but at the same time it needed to be capable of the finest control, so that a great ship could be nudged gently into just the right position. One survivor of the great age of steam tugs is *Portwey*, built at Harland and Wolff in 1927. She has the traditional tug lines: very high in the bow and low in the stern, with a high funnel set just abaft of the wheelhouse. She looks and is powerful, and manœuvrability is improved by the use of twin screws. There are two compound engines, each with a high-pressure and low-pressure cylinder. The boilers are fed from two coal bunkers, one on each side, joined by a cross bunker.

As in other vessels, the steam is used for more than just moving the vessel through the water. It is used, for example, to aid in the steering, for without the assistance of steam power, two men would be needed on the wheel, and *Portwey* only carried a crew of four. She was capable of considerably more than shoving bigger and grander craft into their allotted spaces. A 1918 Robey steam-generator could be used to produce electricity for the vessel, and she carried fire-pumps capable of delivering water at the rate of a ton a minute. And they were not just for use on other vessels: when the Queen's Hotel in Dartmouth caught fire, *Portwey* was on the scene and pumping before the local fire brigade arrived.

But for lovers of ships, her main appeal lies in her role as one of the last of the old breed of marine workhorses, no-nonsense vessels designed to get on with the job in hand with the minimum of fuss. She has none of the conspicuous grace and beauty of the *Cutty Sark*, nor the elegance of a Windermere steam launch. Yet she has that unique appeal that comes from being exactly right for the job in hand, so that it is very good news to hear that when she has steamed off for her last voyage it will not be to the breakers' yard, but to join other historic ships in the Maritime Trust collection.

Portwey is, in many ways, the ideal vessel with which to end this brief survey of historic British ships. Britain has depended on the sea as a protection from invasion, as a route for traders and as a source of food. In recent years, we have also turned increasingly to the sea as a source of pleasure and enjoyment. The Thames barges with which we began started life as purely working boats; today, they are engaged almost exclusively in the new leisure industry. But it is around the working boat, rather than the pleasure boat, that history has been built. So much of our national history is tied up with ships and the sea, that it is rather sad to look at the lists of preserved craft and see so many gaps. Even in the ranks of that most numerous class, the coastal traders, there are vast groups of boats which could have been seen on our waters as recently as half a century ago, but have now disappeared. It is sad that so much has gone, but a comfort that something at least has remained. In 1980 and 1981 I had the great good fortune to put to sea under sail in vessels that first took to the waters as much as a century ago, and to enjoy the unique sight, sound, not to mention smell, of steam. We live in an island community, surrounded by a sea that can be both friend and enemy, but is an ever-present companion. In looking for a demonstration of man's ability to come to terms with his environment, there could be no better example than the work of shipwrights and sailors.

The two triple-expansion engines

It is easy to frown on a preoccupation with the past as a mere pandering to sentimentality. The old sailing ships were beautiful, but their days are done: the coal-fired steamer that inspired Masefield is no more than a rusty anachronism. Some say: the past is over, let it die: the world must change. True, but change does not always come in the ways that we expect. The end of the twentieth century will also see the end of many of our fuel supplies, and in those circumstances we are being forced back to a re-examination of the old ways. Sails are again being seen on commercial vessels: new ways of using coal to raise steam are being investigated. The new sailers and steamers will not look or behave very much like their predecessors, but perhaps the past is not quite so dead as some would have us believe.

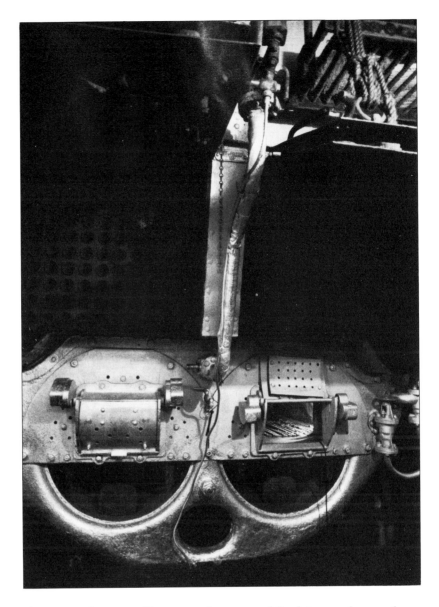

Portwey's multi-tubular boiler and fire boxes. The end of the old age of steam – but is there to be a new steam age?

If it is true that we will never make sense of the future unless we learn to make sense of the past, then perhaps the job of preservation and recording has some value after all. Yet even if there was nothing of the least practical value to be learned from the past, there would still be a case for preserving the best of our old ships. They are the past in which our present was built and, more than that, they have a unique beauty which enriches us all.

Gazetteer

The following is a list of the principal maritime museums and preserved craft in Great Britain

Anstruther, Fife
Scottish Fisheries Museum, Harbour Head
Reaper and *Research* in harbour

Bristol, Avon
SS Great Britain, Great Western Dock, Gas Ferry Road
National Lifeboat Museum, Princes Wharf

Buckler's Hard, Beaulieu, Hampshire
Maritime Museum

Cardiff, South Glamorgan
Welsh Industrial and Maritime Museum, Bute Street
pilot cutter *Kindly Light* and steam tug *Sea Alarm*

Castletown, Isle of Man
Nautical Museum
schooner-rigged yacht *Peggy*, 1791

Coniston, Cumbria
restored steam launch *Gondola*

Cotehele, Cornwall
Maritime Museum, Cotehele Quay
Shamrock

Dundee, Tayside
Victoria Dock
Unicorn

Exeter, Devon
Maritime Museum, The Quay
large collection of vessels from around the world

Falmouth, Cornwall
Barnabas, sailing details, Maritime Trust,
16 Ebury Street, London SW1

Glasgow, Strathclyde
Museum of Transport, 25 Albert Drive
collection of ship models
PS Waverley, sailing details,
Waverley Terminal, Stobcross Quay

Gosport, Hampshire
Submarine Museum
HMS Dolphin and submarine *Alliance*

Great Yarmouth, Norfolk
Maritime Museum for East Anglia, Marine Parade

Hartlepool, Cleveland
Maritime Museum, Northgate
HMS Warrier, Coal Dock

Hull, Humberside
Town Docks Museum, Queen Victoria Square
Maritime museum mainly concerned with fishing
Amy Howson and *Comrade*, sailing details,
Humber Keel and Sloop Preservation Society,
Glenlea, Main Road, New Ellerby, Humberside

Katrine, Loch, Central
SS Sir Walter Scott, regular sailings on Loch
Information from Strathclyde Water Department,
419 Balmore Road, Glasgow

Liverpool, Merseyside
Merseyside Maritime Museum, Pier Head

Lomond, Loch, Strathclyde
PS Maid of the Loch, passenger steamer
Sailing details, Caledonian-MacBrayne,
Ferry Terminal, Gourock, Strathclyde

London
HMS Belfast, Symons Wharf, Vine Lane,
Tooley Street, SE1
Cutty Sark, King William Walk, Greenwich, SE10
Maritime Trust Historic Ship Collection,
St Katharine's by the Tower, E1
National Maritime Museum, Romney Road,
Greenwich, SE10
Science Museum, Exhibition Road, SW1
PS Tattershall Castle, Victoria Embankment, SW1

Morwellham, Devon
Morwellham Quay dock complex and museum on Tamar

Newcastle-upon-Tyne, Tyne and Wear
Science Museum, Exhibition Park
TS Turbinia

Porthmadog, Gwynedd
Maritime Museum, The Harbour
ketch *Garlandstone*

Portsmouth, Hampshire
HMS Victory and Royal Naval Museum,
HM Naval Base

Redcar, Cleveland
Zetland Museum, King Street

Sittingbourne, Kent
Dolphin Yard Sailing Barge Museum, Crown Quay Lane.

Southampton, Hampshire
Maritime Museum, Wool House, Bugle Street

Tarbert, Strathclyde
SS VIC 32, sailing details, *VIC 32*, Crinan,
Lochgilphead, Strathclyde

Thurne, Norfolk
Albion, sailing details, D. E. Anderson,
The Norfolk Wherry Trust, The Croft,
Norwich Road, Lingwood, Norfolk

Windermere, Cumbria
Windermere Steamboat Museum, Rayrigg Road

Further Reading

ANSON, P. F. *Fishing boats and fisher folk on the east coast of Scotland* 1930. Dent, 1971.

BAXTER, J. P. *The introduction of the ironclad warship* OUP, 1933.

BIRD, J. *The major seaports of the United Kingdom* Hutchinson, 1963.

BODY, G. *British paddle steamers* David and Charles, 1971.

BUGLER, A. R. *'H.M.S. Victory': building, restoration and repair* HMSO, 1966.

BUTCHER, D. R. *The driftermen* Tops'l Books, 1979.

CARR, F. G. G. *Sailing barges* 1931. Conway Maritime Press, n.e. 1971.

CORLETT, E. *The iron ship: the history and significance of Brunel's 'Great Britain'* Moonraker Press, 1975.

FINCH, R. *Sailing craft of the British Isles* Collins, 1976.

FLETCHER, H. *A life on the Humber* Faber, 1975.

GREENHILL, B. *The merchant schooners* 1951. National Maritime Museum, n.e. 1978.

GREENHILL, B. ed. *The ship* HMSO for the National Maritime Museum, 1980–81 (10 vols.)

HOLLAND, A. J. *Ships of British oak* David and Charles, 1971.

HYDE, F. E. *Liverpool and the Mersey* David and Charles, 1971.

JOHNSTONE, P. *The sea-craft of prehistory* Routledge and Kegan Paul, 1980.

KEMP, P. *The history of ships* Orbis Books, 1978.

KEMP, P. *The Oxford companion to ships and the sea* OUP, 1976.

LENTON, H. T. *British submarines* Macdonald, 1972.

LONGRIDGE, C. N. *The 'Cutty Sark'* Model and Allied Publications, 1975.

LYON, D. J. and H. J. L. *World War II warships* Orbis Books, 1976.

MCDONALD, D. *The Clyde puffer* David and Charles, 1977.

MACGREGOR, D. R. *Clipper ships* Argus Books, 1979.

MALSTER, R. *Wherries and waterways* Dalton, 1971.

MARCH, E. J. *Sailing drifters* 1952. David and Charles, 1969.

NATIONAL MARITIME MUSEUM *Three major ancient boat finds in Britain* The Museum, 1972.

PATERSON, A. J. S. *The golden years of the Clyde steamers 1889–1914* David and Charles, 1969.

RITCHIE-NOAKES, N. *Jesse Hartley* Merseyside County Museums, 1980.

SLADE, W. J. and GREENHILL, B. *Westcountry coasting ketches* Conway Maritime Press, 1974.

UDEN, G. and COOPER, R. *A dictionary of British ships and seamen* Kestrel Books, 1980.

UNGER, R. W. *The ship in the medieval economy, 600–1600* Croom Helm, 1980.

WATTS, A. J. *Allied submarines* Macdonald and Jane's, 1977.

Glossary

Adze
A cutting tool with a blade set at right angles to the shaft, used for shaping ships' timbers.

Aftercastle
Originally a structure built up on the stern of a man of war to hold armament.

Beak
A projecting structure at the bows of sixteenth- and seventeenth-century ships, so called because it resembles the beak of a bird.

Beam
Part of the framework of a ship (see fig. 2). The width of a vessel amidships, hence 'beam ratio', the ratio of beam to length.

Block
A pulley or pulleys mounted in a case, designed to guide a rope and increase pulling power.

Boom
A spar used to extend the foot of a sail. Also a floating barrier at the entrance to a harbour

Bow
The forward end of a vessel.

Bowsprit
A sprit which runs out from the bow of a ship which supports sails such as jib sails (see fig. 1).

Brail
To furl a sail by pulling it in towards the mast.

Capstan
A rotating cylinder, used for hauling cable, especially the anchor cable.

1 Jigger or spanker
2 Jigger gaff topsail
3 Mizzen topmast staysail
4 Mizzen staysail
5 Main royal sail
6 Main top gallant sail
7 Main upper topsail
8 Main lower topsail
9 Main sail
10 Main top gallant staysail
11 Main topmast staysail
12 Fore royal sail
13 Fore top gallant sail
14 Fore upper topsail
15 Fore lower topsail
16 Foresail
17 Fore topmast staysail
18 Inner jib
19 Outer jib
20 Flying jib

Carvel-built
Describes a vessel in which the outer planks of the hull lie flush with each other, and are attached to a previously constructed frame.

Caulk
To make a ship watertight by forcing oakum into the cracks, then covering the seams with pitch.

Centre board
A plate which is dropped through a slot in the bottom of a boat to prevent the boat slipping sideways in the water. Also known as a drop keel.

Cleat
A fixture of wood or metal on a boat around which a rope can be secured.

Clew
The lower corner of a square sail; the aftermost lower corner of a fore and aft sail (see fig. 4).

Clinker- (or clench-) built
Describes a vessel in which the hull is constructed from overlapping planks.

Coaming
The raised edge round a hatch.

Dumb barge
A barge with no power of its own, which is either towed or floats with tide and current.

Fathom
A depth measurement of six feet.

Fore and aft rig
A rig in which sails lie along the fore and aft axis of the ship, that is on the line between bow and stern.

Forecastle (fo'c'sle)
Originally the built up area in the bows of a man of war to hold armament; later the foremost part of the deck, below which merchant seamen had their quarters.

Foremast
The mast of a vessel which stands nearest the bows (see fig. 1).

Futtock
Part of the main frame of a wooden ship (see fig. 2). Also futtock plate on the mast to which rigging is attached, and futtock shrouds, rigging that runs down from the futtock plate to the mast.

Gaff
The spar which holds the upper edge of a four-sided fore and aft sail.

Gunwale
The upper part of a ship's side.

Halyard
A rope or tackle for hoisting a spar holding a sail.

Jib sail
A triangular sail, normally extending from bowsprit to foremast (see fig. 1).

Keel
The lowest timber or iron member of a ship's frame on which the rest of the frame is constructed (see fig. 2). Also a square rigged, shallow draught coaster.

Keelson
A timber or iron plate above the keel (see fig. 2).

Knee
A bent timber, securing beams to ribs of wooden ships or, in later vessels, an angular iron piece performing the same function (see fig. 2).

Knot
The unit of measurement of a ship's speed, defined as one nautical mile per hour. A nautical mile is 1·15 land miles, so that a ship travelling at 20 knots would be moving at 23 m.p.h.

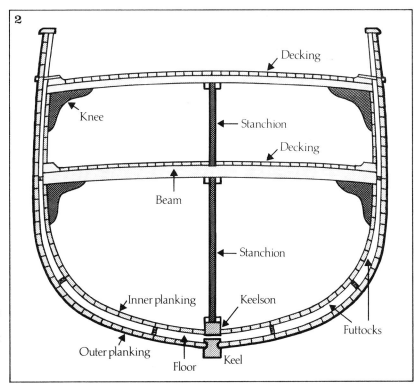

2

Decking

Knee

Stanchion

Decking

Beam

Stanchion

Inner planking

Keelson

Futtocks

Outer planking

Floor

Keel

Lateen sail
A triangular sail, used in Mediterranean and Middle Eastern craft.

Lee boards
Triangular or pear shaped boards which can be lowered over the sides of shallow draught sailing vessels to prevent them slipping sideways in the water.

Leech
The side edge of a square sail, or the after edge of a fore and aft sail (see fig. 4).

Luff
The forward edge of a fore and aft sail (see fig. 4); also to sail a ship closer to the wind.

Lug sail
A four sided sail hung from a yard in which the halyard is set closer to the forward end. In a dipping lug, the yard is dipped and carried round the mast in tacking.

Mainmast
The principal mast in a vessel (see fig. 1).

Mizzen
The aftermost mast in a three masted vessel; the mast aft of the mainmast in a two masted vessel (see fig. 1).

Molgogger
A portable device with rollers fastened to the side of a fishing vessel through which the warp is run out.

Peak
The uppermost corner of a fore and aft sail (see fig. 4).

Poop
The raised section at the stern of a ship, developed from the aftercastle.

Reef
To shorten a sail by rolling up the bottom section and securing it by short lines attached to the sails.

3

Rigging
The general name for ropes, chains, wires etc. which hold masts, spars and yards in place. Standing rigging is permanently fixed; running rigging controls the movement of sails and spars.

Scarf
A joint between two timbers (see fig. 3).

Seizing
The line attaching the bottom of a drift net to the warp (see fig. 6).

Sheet
A line running from the bottom aft corner of a sail by which the sail can be adjusted to the wind (see fig. 5).

Shrouds
Standing rigging running up from the sides of a ship to support the masts.

Snotter
A hoop or collar passing round a mast, holding the foot of a sprit.

Sprit
A spar running diagonally upwards from the mast to the aft, upper corner of a fore and aft sail, hence spritsail.

Square rig
Rig consisting of four cornered sails hung from a yard set athwartships.

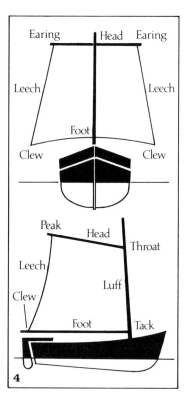

4

Stay
Standing rigging supporting a mast and running fore and aft. Sails hung from the stays are staysails (see fig. 1).

Stern
The after end of a vessel.

Strake
A line of planking running from bow to stern, forming part of a vessel's side.

Strop
The line attaching the top of a drift net to a buoy (see fig. 6).

Studding sail (stunsail)
Sail extending out beyond the side edge of a square sail to make the most of light winds.

Swim
The overhanging part of the bow or stern.

Tabernackle
A deck socket in which a mast rests, held in place by a pin. When the pin is removed, the mast can be raised or lowered.

Tack
Lower, forward corner of a fore and aft sail (see fig. 4). In square rigged ships, the line controlling the forward lower corner of a sail when sailing toward the wind. (see fig. 5). Also the ship's course in relation to the wind, so that if the wind is coming from the port or starboard side so the ship is said to be on a port or starboard tack.

Thole
A pair of wooden pins set on the gunwale to act as the pivot point for an oar.

Throat
The upper forward corner of a fore and aft sail (see fig. 4). Also the end of a gaff adapted to fit round the mast.

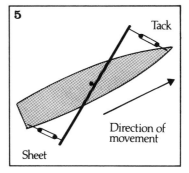

Treenail
A wooden peg used in hull construction.

Truck
The wooden disc at the top of a mast.

Tumblehome
The curve of a hull which makes the upper deck of a vessel narrower than the deck near the waterline.

Vang
Running rigging, securing the end of a gaff or sprit.

Warp
A rope or cable used to move a vessel; the rope or wire used for hauling a fishing net (see fig. 5).

Whipstaff
A device in the form of a lever, used before the introduction of the steering wheel to move the rudder.

Yard
A spar attached to a mast to carry a sail.

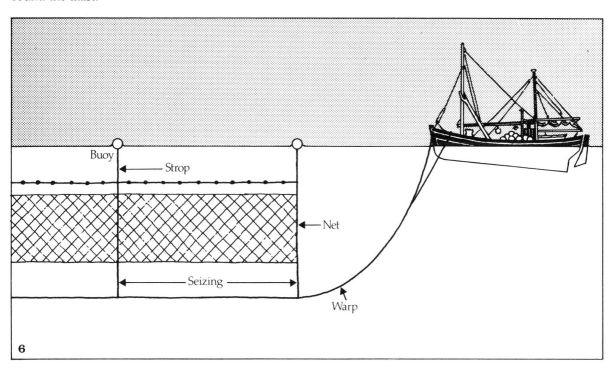

Index

A

Adams, Henry, 131–2
Adventurer, 123
Agamemnon, 128, 130, 131
Albion, 44–9
Alecto, 77
Alliance, 160–3
Amy Howson, 39–40
Anderson, Ewan, 46
Anglia, 54–5
Ann McKim, 64
Anson, Admiral George, 132
Archimedes, 77, 85
Armament
  cannon, 133–8, 141
  guns, rifled, 145–6, 149
  torpedos, 160, 162
  turrets, 151, 153–4
Ayton, Richard, 175

B

Barnabas, 43
Belfast, 152–7, 163
Bell, Henry, 71
Blase, Sir Gilbert, 143
Brandon, 90
British Museum, 14
Brown, Basil, 16
Brunel, Isambard Kingdom, 83–9, 91
Buckler's Hard, 128-32
Burns, Robert, 68, 70
Bushnell, David, 158

C

Calstock, 167
Cap Norte, 154
Caravels, 57
Carracks, 57
Carron ironworks, 134
Charlestown, 166
Charlotte Dundas, 71
Chatham, 133, 140
Clermont, 71
Collier, 96
Columbus, Christopher, 57
Comet, 71–2, 73, 74
Comrade, 29–40, 43
Cordes, James, 96
Cotehele, 167–9
Cutty Sark, 63–70

D

d'Abbans, Claude de Jouffroy, 70
de Caux, J. W., 107, 108
de Lôme, Dupuy, 145–6
Demolgos, 145
Devonport, 167
Dodd, Henry, 9, 55
Dolly, 77–81, 94
Dolphin Yard Museum, 22–7
Downman, Captain Wilfred, 67
Dreadnought, 101
Drifters, 109–19
Duchess of York, 72

E

Ericsson, John, 77, 145, 151

F

Falconer, William, 132, 140
Ferriby boats, 12–15, 19, 23–4
Fitch, John, 70
Francis Smith, 77
Fulton, Robert, 71, 145, 158

G

Gillow, Richard, 170
Gillow, Robert, 169
Gloire, 146, 148
Grâce Dieu, 20
Graveney boat, 18–19
Great Britain, 81, 85–9, 91, 103
Great Western, 83, 85
Greathead, Henry, 123, 125

H

Hardwick, Philip, 175
Hartley, Jesse, 175
Hawkins, Sir John, 127
Hero of Alexandria, 96
Hillary, Sir William, 125
Hornblower, Jonathan, 89
Housatonic, 159
Hull construction
  armoured, 148–9
  carvel, 20–2
  clinker, 17–20, 29
  composite, 67, 141
  early, 9–22
  iron, 85
Humphreys, Francis, 85

Hutchison, Lieutenant-Commander,
  J. K. D., 16

J

John Bowes, 96

K

Kathleen and May, 58–61, 95–6, 169

L

Lancaster, 169–70
Leptis Magna, 165
Lifeboats, 123–5
Linton, Hercules, 68
Liverpool, 172–9
Locke, Edward, 96
Lowestoft, 107
Lukin, Lionel, 123, 125
Lydia Eva, 114–19

M

Manxman, 103–4
Maritime Trust, 59, 95–6, 115–16, 149
Mauretania, 103
Merrimack, 151
Mevagissey, 165
Miller, Patrick, 90
Moffat, Cleveland, 100
Mona's Isle, 103
Monitor, 151
Montagu, Duke of, 130–1
Morwellham, 167

N

Napoléon, 146
National Maritime Museum, 14, 17,
  19, 168, 169
National Trust, 168
Nelson, Admiral Horatio, 128, 131–3,
  138
Nonsuch, 114
Normand, Benjamin, 92
Normandie, 103

O

Original, 123
Otto, 94

P
Paixhams, Henry-Joseph, 145
Parsons, Sir Charles, 96–101
Pattinson, George, 21–2
Périer, J. C., 70
Phillips, Charles, 13
Polperro, 165
Port Isaac, 165
Portwey, 179
Prince Albert, 151
Pyroscaphe, 70

Q
Queen Elizabeth, 103
Queen Mary, 103

R
Rafts, 12
Rattler, 77
Reaper, 110–14
Research, 114
Revival, 25–7
Roberts, Thomas, 140
Robin, 95–6
Royal George, 133
Royal National Lifeboat Institution, 125
Rumsey, James, 70
Russell, John Scott, 146

S
Sailing vessels,
    gaff rig, 40–2, 44–9
    ketch, 167–9
    lateen, 57
    lugger, 43, 110, 114
    schooner, 57–61
    spritsail, 9, 22–7, 49–55
    square rig, 29–40, 63–70, 132–43
St Katherine's Dock, 59, 95–6, 115, 175
Scharnhorst, 157
Schofield, Fred, 39
Science Museum, London, 16, 71, 98
Science Museum, Newcastle-upon-Tyne, 98
Scott, William Dundas, 68
Scottish Fisheries Museum, 110, 119–22
Shamrock, 169
Shipbuilding, 22–7, 59–60, 128–32

Sirius, 83
Slade, Sir Thomas, 133
Smeaton, John, 166
Smith, Francis Pettit, 77, 85, 145
Spithead Review, 100–1
Steamers
    paddle, 70–7, 83, 85, 145
    screw, simple, 77–81, 85–9, 91
    screw, compound, 89–92, 179
    screw, triple expansion, 92–6, 115
    screw, turbine, 96–104
Steers, Thomas, 172
Submarine, 157–63
Submarine Museum, 160
Sutton Hoo boat, 13, 15–19
Swallow, 94
Symington, William, 70–1

T
Telford, Thomas, 175
Thermopylae, 64
Thomas W. Lawson, 61
Trawlers, 109
Trevithick, Richard, 96
Turbinia, 97–101
Turtle, 158

U
Unicorn, 140–3
United States, 103

V
VIC 32, 90–2, 103
Victory, 132–40, 149
Viper, 101
Vital Spark, 91

W
Warrior, 146–51
Watts, Sir Isaac, 146
Waverley, 73–7
Whitehead, Robert, 160
Wilkinson, John, 85
Windermere Steamboat Museum, 21–2, 77–81, 94–6
Woodget, Captain Richard, 65
Woolf, Arthur, 89
Wouldhave, William, 123
Wright, C. W., 13
Wright, E. V., 13–15

Y
Yarmouth, 107–8

Z
Zetland, 123–5

Ballet Beginnings
for Children

Pre-School
Movement Fundamentals
Ages 3 and 4

Music to accompany these classes are on 2 CDs bound inside the back cover of this book.
The exercises in this book are presented on the DVD *A Fantasy Garden Ballet Class I and II*.

This delightful program will engage children three and four years old
who are not yet ready for ballet and prepare them for pre-ballet.

A Fantasy Garden Ballet Class, DVDs I and II, may be ordered separately from
Princeton Book Company, Publishers, 614 Route 130, Hightstown, New Jersey 08520
1-800-220-7149
www.dancehorizons.com

Ballet Beginnings
for Children

Pre-School
Movement Fundamentals
Ages 3 and 4

Rosemary Boross

2 Music CDs Included

Princeton Book Company, Publishers
Hightstown, New Jersey

Design and illustrations by John McMenamin
Coloring pages drawings by Rosemary Boross
Cover design by Connie Woodford

Publisher's Cataloging-In-Publication Data
(Prepared by The Donohue Group, Inc.)

Boross, Rosemary
   Ballet beginnings for children : pre-school movement fundamentals ages 3 and 4 /
Rosemary Boross.
   XXX p. : XXX ill. ; XXX cm. + 1 sound disc

   "Music CDs included."
   ISBN-13: 978-0-87127-289-8
   ISBN-10: 0-87127-289-X

1. Ballet--Study and teaching (Preschool) 2. Ballet dancing--Handbooks, manuals, etc.
I. Title.

GV1788.5 .B67 2007
792.8

Princeton Book Company, Publishers
614 Route 130
Hightstown, NJ 08520
www.dancehorizons.com

Contents

Introduction   1

  The Contents of a Pre-school Class   2

    Choosing appropriate movements   2

    Formulating the class   3

    Warm-up   4

    Center work   4

    Across the floor   4

    Creative movement   4

    Réverénce   4

  Methods of Teaching Very Young Children   5

    Props   5

    Imagery   6

    Games   7

    Music   7

    Assistants   7

    Teaching the class   7

A Fantasy Garden Ballet Class Part I   9

  Warm-up Exercises   9

    The Sun   10

    It's Morning   16

    I'm a Butterfly   18

    Mr. Inchworm   21

    I'm A Big Oak Tree   27

    Coupé the Cricket   30

Center Floor Exercises   34

    Tendu the Tulip   34

    Port de bras the Spider   40

    Skippy the Squirrel   44

    Chassé the Chipmunk (1, 2 and 3 claps)   48

    Échappé Azalea   55

    Bourrée the Bee   58

    Sauté the Bunny   62

    Pas de Chat the Pansy   66

    Plié the Poppy   69

    Creative movement   71

    Révérence   72

A Fantasy Garden Ballet Class Part II

    Center Floor Exercises   75

    Emboîté Ants   76

    Mr. Robin Red Breast   78

    Friendly Frogs   81

    Leaping Ladybugs   83

    Green, Green, Galloping Grasshoppers   85

    The Caterpillar Circle   87

    Prancing Petunias   90

    Marching Marigolds   92

Coloring Pages   94

Disk Programs   120

Introduction

The pre-school classes in this book are created especially for children three and four years old. They are designed to make learning ballet—its terminology, movements and traditions—fun and easy.

The book is structured to help dance teachers using a well-tested format. It is also for parents who want to know what their child should be learning in his or her beginning years of dance. It contains ideas on the fundamentals of teaching very young students, levels of training, helpful material and class exercises that can be used for movement fundamentals. I feel that training young students is of the utmost importance. Since these are their formative years, it is essential that children be pointed in the right direction. Early training will give them a strong basis that will prepare them for their future in ballet.

Teaching students who are three and four years old is very different from teaching older students. Since they are so young, they do not have the muscular coordination, concentration or ability to understand the complexity of technique taught in a standard ballet class. What should their training include? How should you develop their young bodies? How do you convey to them the spiritual aspects of dance and instill a love and respect for dance? What encourages their hunger to learn? Most importantly, how can you prepare them for ballet technique without physically harming them?

The goal for teaching ballet fundamentals with good basic technique should the same for students of all ages. How do we go about helping younger students achieve these goals? A long, slow, repetitive class will not hold their interest or inspire them to want to dance. So what do we teach them? How do we inspire them? How do we make them physically ready and motivate them to proceed to the next level? There is no standardized ballet class to follow for this age group. Teaching young students is both a complex and a challenging task.

The key lies in how you choose to present the appropriate fundamentals at the appropriate level for your students.

The Contents of a Pre-school Class

For ages three and four, a 30- to 45-minute class is sufficient. The class should include stretching and strengthening exercises that are repeated often enough to train their bodies without being physically harmful. They must learn the importance of dance technique and what it is. They must also be gently taught the discipline that is involved in a dance class and the importance of adhering to it. This might sound overwhelming for such young children, but it can all be accomplished when class is presented to them at their level of comprehension and physicality.

Choosing appropriate movements

It is important that students are not asked to execute intricate movements requiring coordination and concentration beyond their capabilities. Demands that are too strong and overwhelming will cause frustration and kill both the class's momentum and the student's enthusiasm. Students should work on basic movements that they can master and that will give them a sense of accomplishment. Pre-school ballet training should be an introduction to fundamental movements executed with spatial design, creativity and musicality, beginning with the following:

1) Exercises to develop an awareness of movement capabilities in back, legs, feet and arms

2) Exercises to develop flexibility, strength and coordination

3) Refinement of basic motor skills

4) Creative development

5) Spatial instruction (right, left, forward, backward)

6) Spatial designs (circles, lines, diagonals)

7) Musical sensitivity (dynamics and rhythm)

8) Aerobic activity

Ballet steps that incorporate basic motor skills and fundamental movements are:
Plié to straight legs, executed with dynamics and rhythm which
teaches musicality.

Chassé, the basic motor skill of galloping, teaches spatial awareness and
directional skills.

Sautés such as skipping, lifting the legs and knees high, develops strength and
elevation, which in turn provides aerobic exercise.

Relevés and *bourrées* will be executed automatically when the student is
asked to reach up as high as she can or to imitate a bird flying in the sky.

Leaps teach spatial awareness and dynamics. Spring points and
pas de chats will develop coordination and balance.

Grand jetés, simply running and jumping over an object, will teach the
dynamics of force and use of space.

Jumps with two feet, using spatial direction with an emphasis on elevation,
again provide aerobic activity and will strengthen the legs.

Port de bras develops balance, coordination, grace, and form—an awareness
of the shapes that the arms can make.

Although you might be using ballet steps, *the use of turn-out is not necessary for
this age group.* At this age, turn-out is potentially harmful. They are too young to understand how to correctly hold turn-out with proper alignment and they do not have the muscular development to execute it. It is best to work in parallel, using a natural position of the legs.

Repetition is also important to develop muscular strength and endurance. Repetition can be accomplished by combining the same basic movements with different concepts and imagery.

Formulating the class

A pre-school class should be designed much like formal dance class. Begin with warm-up and continue on to center work and across the floor. This way, the students will begin to learn the discipline and the basic structure of a dance class.

Warm-up

The warm-up should include activities that will focus on the entire body: feet, legs, hips, neck, torso and arms. During the warm-up, the student should begin to develop awareness of the movement capabilities of the different parts of his or her body. Gentle stretching and strengthening should be included.

Center work

Center work should include movements that will develop coordination, strength and balance while working on spatial movement (right, left, front and back) and spatial designs (circles, lines). Have the students work as a group or with a partner so they learn to share the space with their fellow students. They will learn to work together as they create spatial relationships and spatial designs with one another.

Across the floor

In this section of class, the students are taught how to work individually. They will learn to move through the space, creating designs on their own. While doing so, they will use movement dynamics that include changes of energy and spatial levels. Across-the-floor work teaches students the basic discipline of waiting for their turn and provides an opportunity for them to learn how to show respect for fellow students.

Creative movement

This is usually the favorite part of the class, when students are free to explore and create their own movement. It is a good time to develop their musical sensitivity by using music with varied dynamics and beats. They will begin to develop understanding of the use of movement dynamics in relationship to the music.

Révérence

Révérence, signaling the end of class, is one of the most time-honored traditions in ballet. It must be taken seriously, as it is the time when the children will come to learn that they have just accomplished something very special. *Révérence* includes a curtsey to say goodbye to the teacher, applause for a job well done and lots of praise. Ending the class in a positive manner will instill an excitement in the students who will then look forward to returning to their next class.

Methods of Teaching Very Young Children

When teaching this age group, everything needs to be fun. If the students are happy, they will be very enthusiastic, and in turn, they will learn faster. Children love to play, so the use of props, imagery and games can be very helpful. The music used should be child-related. You may use songs with lyrics which can be acted out or songs to which they can sing along.

I have had the opportunity to meet with many teachers, having taught at teacher seminars for many dance organizations over the years, and some have shared their ideas with me. One teacher uses small traffic cones while her students pretend to be cars in traffic. This is her tool for teaching spatial design and direction. Another teacher I met cultivates her students' graceful ballet walks by having them walk with beanbags on their heads while standing very tall. Games as simple as *Ring Around the Rosie* teach circular directions. Putting on special ballet skirts or tutus and pretending to be ballerinas sparks creativity. So does dancing around a hat to the *Mexican Hat Dance.* Teachers can make a student feel special by appointing her or him as the teacher for a certain exercise. Other creative activities are having students dance with dolls or pretend to be taffy stretching.

I have found that possibilities are endless when using these kinds of tools. I chose to develop my class with a garden theme and before I knew it, I had designed an entire class around that theme. With a little imagination, I came up with all sorts of activities incorporating props, imagery, games and music. Here is a sampling of some of them:

Props

For my garden theme class, I cut mats into the shape of flowers and painted them bright colors. On the other side of the mats, I painted lily pads. These mats served many purposes throughout the class. The students could choose their own flower, which was very exciting for them. They learned to share flowers with their fellow classmates from week to week. The mats kept the children in their own spaces, sitting or standing on their own flowers throughout the warm-up. I used the flowers as a reference point while teaching spatial directions. I would instruct the students to move to the right, left, forward and back of the flowers and to circle the flowers to the right or to the left. We used the flowers to explore spatial designs, placing them in different patterns on the floor and dancing around and over them. They were useful when teaching leaps, as the students would go leaping from one flower to another or leap over their own. We used the lily pad to work on jumping while pretending to be frogs.

Other props have worked equally well in the garden-theme class. We danced with scarves and bouquets of flowers when doing creative movement. I have made laminated pictures of garden flora and fauna and hung them on the mirrors with suction-cupped hooks. Each character was named to coincide with the step that was taught that day. Such characters as Pas de Chat the Pansy, Skippy the Squirrel, and Tendu the Tulip helped my students learn the terminology of the steps. They also came in handy when the children were tired and needed a break. We could color pictures of the characters.

Imagery

During warm-up, we pretended to be different objects or situations in a garden. Each warm-up would tell a story about that object or situation.

Using the story of how a flower grows is a good example: flowers need sun to grow, so we become the sun way up in the sky. While sitting on the floor with our legs straight out in front, we made a circle with our arms overhead and reached for the sky. This taught fifth position of the arms and elongation of the back. We showed how the rays of sun come down and warm the ground and the seeds. This helped students stretch their backs and legs while reaching forward to stroke the ground. Their feet were the seeds that need to be warmed up. As students reached for their feet, they got an even more intense stretch. We then pretended to be the rain in the clouds that float in the sky, reaching up (again elongating the back) and swaying right and left to warm up the torso. We came back down to the floor again, pretending to be the raindrops coming down from the clouds to water the seeds. We made the sound of the raindrops with our fingertips on the floor for further stretching. The seeds woke up, came alive, and danced. As the seeds danced around, they learned the articulations of the feet by flexing and pointing. They also warmed up their ankles by circling them.

The remainder of the class continued to follow the theme. The students pretended to be butterflies as they stretched and warmed up their hips and inchworms for an overall body strengthening exercise. We created a fantasy garden that lasted the entire class.

Games

In the creative movement section, we played tag. Students were divided equally among the four corners of the room, with four children in the center. I turned on the pre-set music and the four students in the center began to dance. When the music changed, they ran to a corner and tagged the next set of dancers to come out and dance. The game went on until everyone had a turn.

The game taught them sensitivity to music since they had to listen for the musical changes. They learned to follow directions and take turns. They enjoyed exploring their own creativity and learned how to move with the dynamics of the music.

Music

Although there is a lot of children's music available today that will inspire and motivate younger students, I created my own music for this class. I wrote the lyrics and called upon a composer friend of mine to write the music. The lyrics helped the children to remember what comes next in an exercise, and they loved to sing along. The music for *A Fantasy Garden Ballet Class, Parts I and II* is on the CDs in the inside back cover of this book. I hope you find it as useful as I have!

Assistants

I find that it is very helpful to have one of my young adult advanced students assisting in the class. As I teach, my assistant can move around from student to student and give them hands-on corrections. An assistant is especially important if the class is large, as she or he can help you to keep order in the class.

Teaching the class

The teacher's demeanor and how she or he relates to the students are both very important. The teacher is their role model and they will imitate everything that the teacher does. Here are some things that a teacher should be aware of when teaching this age group:

1. Prepare ahead of time. When the lesson plan is well thought out, the teacher can keep the class moving at a good pace and make sure that there is no idle time when the student's attention might be lost.

2. Get into it. The teacher's enthusiasm will be sensed by the students and will keep everyone inspired.

3. Care. The teacher should show that she cares about each student individually. Learn who is who quickly and always call students by their names.

4. Keep your words concise; do not use lengthy explanations. Explanations should be limited from the beginning or the children will become bored. Explain the how and the why of each exercise in a little more detail each week as the class progresses.

5. Be light. Corrections should be kept short, simple and lighthearted. For instance, if someone is not pointing his or her toes, the teacher can simply say, "Oops, are we all pointing our toes?"

6. Be positive. Praise is essential to keep students motivated. During class, bring attention to each child by name and point out something that she or he has done correctly, no matter how small it may seem.

7. Dance with them. The teacher should always demonstrate exercises or steps so that students can simply dance along. At this age, they learn by imitating.

8. Set an example. You are furthering a centuries-old tradition! The appearance of the teacher is important and she or he should wear the proper dress for a ballet class (leotard or shirt, skirt or black tights, neat hair).

9. Be clear. Teachers should share their thoughts with the students about a particular exercise. Students respond better when they understand the reason why they are doing it.

10. Be specific. The teacher should break down the steps adequately and simply so that the students can see and understand the movement easily.

A Fantasy Garden Ballet Class Part I

Warm-up Exercises

In the classes that follow, there is enough material to complete an entire year of training. Also included are variations of many of the exercises and suggestions for the students' advancement. The goals of each exercise, how to present it and the principles involved are given, along with basic corrections and common mistakes to watch for—as it is important to be consistent in reinforcing the corrections to achieve good basic technique. Classes include a warm-up, stretching and strengthening exercises, and movement fundamentals like basic motor skills and creative movement. There are variations given for many of the exercises and suggestions for student advancement.

The basic ballet movements and steps are associated with appealing flower and animal characters that make it easy and fun for young students to remember each movement and its name in ballet terminology.

A most important factor in the warm-up exercises is the repetition of movement, which children need to gain flexibility and strength. Because the characters and stories constantly change, they are not aware of repetition and less likely to become bored or distracted. They love to sing along as they perform the exercises, which in turn help them to remember all of the movements. They enjoy acting out various garden situations as flowers grow, bees buzz from flower to flower and birds fly around a big oak tree.

Keep in mind that it is important to be consistent in reinforcing the corrections. Constant positive reinforcement will help students achieve good basic technique at a faster pace.

The exercises in this section are presented on the DVD *A Fantasy Garden Ballet Class I*
and on the music CD, *A Fantasy Garden Ballet Class Volume I*,
bound inside the back cover of this book.

The Sun
Variations 1 and 2

Goals
Variation 1

Elongate spine.

Achieve fifth position of the arms.

Stretch hamstrings.

Stretch and warm up torso.

Articulate feet.

Warm up feet and ankles.

Variation 2

Intensely warm up legs.

Intensely warm up feet and ankles.

Correctly execute directional movement (turning right and left).

Presentation and principles
Variation 1

Referring to the body parts used in this exercise will produce a quick response from students to corrections and reinforcement of technique:

Our arms are the sun, way up in the sky, and they elongate the spine as we practice fifth position of the arms.

Our arms are the rays of the sun coming down. The rays stroke the ground near and on the seeds (which are our feet) to warm the ground and stretch our legs.

Our arms are the rain as they reach up to the sky and stretch the torso upward. Our wiggling fingers are the raindrops.

The raindrops come down and have to water the seeds, giving a more intense stretch. The children enjoy tapping their fingers on the ground to make the sound of the raindrops.

The seeds wake up (flex and point) and dance around (circling ankles) to create an awareness and articulation of the feet.

Variation 2

In this variation the arms are again the sun and the rain. Since we travel from a standing position to a squatting position, reaching up to the sky includes use of the feet in *relevé*. The legs benefit from a more intense stretch as they straighten and stretch to a further extreme than in the first variation.

When the seeds wake up, the torso's gentle bouncing warms up and stretches the legs, feet, and ankles.

Learn the directions of turns (right and left) while dancing around on our toes.

Correcting common mistakes

Variation 1

Straighten knees while stretching.

Point the feet.

Stretch arms and back as high as they can reach in the high fifth position.

Keep shoulders down.

Encourage the feet to make big movements when flexing, pointing and circling.

Variation 2

Reach high to achieve a high *relevé* while stretching and strengthening legs.

Keep knees directly over feet (the seeds) when squatting.

Bounce torso gently to create small, controlled movement.

Work continually toward getting students to turn in the directions you have set when dancing around on their toes. This will take some time—just be consistent with the correction.

Advancement

Variations 1 and 2

This exercise needs to be performed in every class for students to achieve maximum flexibility and strength. Once the students have mastered the first variation, go on to the second. Continue to teach both variations, one time each, consecutively.

Switch from the vocal version of the music to the instrumental version once the students know the exercise.

The Sun

Variation 1

 1 Begin sitting on the floor with the legs outstretched in front of you. Toes should be pointed and the back should be elongated, sitting very tall.

 2 The sun comes out up in the sky,

The arms come up to fifth position with the back still elongated and the toes still pointed.

 3 The rays come down and warm the ground.

Bend and stretch forward and stroke the floor and the feet.

 4 I see our friend, Mr. Rain, floating in the clouds so high,

Reach the arms up over head to an elongated back. Begin to wiggle the fingers and sway right and left from the waist.

 5 He starts to fall gently down to the ground, lightly pitter–pattering all around.

Bend and stretch forward, tapping the floor and the feet with the fingers.

 6 The seeds wake up and come alive

Sit up with an elongated back, flexing and pointing the feet.

 7 And dance around and round and round and round and round.

Continue sitting with an elongated back while circling the feet from the ankles.

Variation 2

 1 Begin in a squatting position with the hands on the floor.

 2 The sun comes out up in the sky.

Come up to a standing position with the arms in fifth position overhead and the feet in *relevé*, up on the toes.

 3 The rays come down and warm the ground.

Come back down to the squatting position with the hands on the floor and stroke the ground.

 4 I see our friend Mr. Rain floating in the clouds so high.

Come back to the standing position, reaching the arms up overhead wiggling the fingers. Begin to bend right and left from the waist. The feet are in *relevé*, up on the toes, while taking quick little *bourrée* steps.

 5 He starts to fall, gently down to the ground.

Come back down to the squatting position again, while the fingers tap on the ground around you and on the feet, making the sounds of the raindrops.

 6 The seeds wake up and come alive

In the squatting position, begin bouncing gently from the knees up and down.

 7 And dance around and round and round and round and round.

Come up to a standing position with the arms in fifth position overhead. The feet are in *relevé* up on the toes. Begin taking tiny *bourrée* steps on the toes while turning around.

As the music ends, come back down to the squatting position with the hands on the floor.

It's Morning

Goals

Warm up the back.

Achieve the second position stretch.

Stretch the hamstrings.

Stretch the sides of the torso.

Strengthen the abdominals.

Achieve *port de bras* fifth, second, and *allongé* positions.

Warm up legs and feet.

Warm up and stretch inner thighs.

Presentation and principles

Referring to the body parts used in this exercise will produce a quick response from students to corrections and reinforcement of technique:

Our legs are the petals and our feet are the seeds of a flower. We need to keep our petals straight and point our seeds throughout the exercise. This will reinforce the technique of pulling up in the legs and pointing the toes throughout a movement.

In second position, we need to keep our petals (knees) facing the sun because a flower needs the sun to grow. This will assure a technically correct second position of the legs.

When the rays of the sun come down, we also warm our seeds (feet). This will help students to achieve their maximum stretch.

The arms in high fifth are the sun in the sky. Reaching the arms way up to the sky will achieve a tall back and fully stretched arms in the high fifth position.

The sleeping position simulates a flower closing its petals when the sun goes down. Students use inner thighs and abdominals muscles to slowly close their petals with straight legs.

Using the imagery of the chill in the air when the sun goes down will help the students to hold a tight position when rocking themselves to sleep.

Correcting common mistakes

Keep knees straight while stretching.

Point the feet.

Keep both hips on the floor while stretching to the side in second position.

Lengthen the spine and arms while dropping shoulders in high fifth.

Rotate knees upward while in second position.

Advancement

This exercise needs to be performed in every class for the students to achieve maximum flexibility. Begin by doing the exercise only once. Incorporate repetition once the students are able to do the exercise with proper technique.

Switch to using the instrumental version of the music once the students know the exercise.

It's Morning

1 Begin sitting with the knees tucked tightly to the chest and the arms wrapped tightly around the legs. The head is bent down and forward to the knees and the toes are pointed.

2 It's morning, it's morning, It's time to wake up.

Stretch the legs straight forward, while keeping the feet pointed. Stretch the arms and the body up and out while yawning.

3 I stretch my petals as far as they'll go.

Place the hands on the floor behind you. Keeping the legs straight and the toes pointed, open the legs to second position. Then open the arms to second position.

4 And then the wind begins to blow.

Begin to stretch from the waist right and left, keeping the legs straight, toes pointed and the arms stretching over the head, reaching side to side toward the feet.

5 It blows me to the front.

Stretch forward from the hips, trying to lay flat on the floor with the arms overhead. The legs remain straight in second position, toes pointed.

6 It blows me to the right, it blows me to the left.

While staying low to the ground, reach and stretch over the right leg reaching for the right foot. Repeat this to the left while the legs remain straight with the toes pointed.

7 And then the sun comes out so bright.

Sit up with an elongated back with the arms overhead in fifth position.

8 It feels so good, it feels so warm.

Open the arms to second position, then *allongé* and place the hands just behind the legs.

9 I stretch my petals a little bit more.

Using the hands against the floor, lift the hips up slightly and push the hips forward to open up the second position a little bit wider.

 10 And lay around in the sun.

Reach forward from the hips, trying to keep them flat on the floor with the arms overhead. The legs remain straight, toes pointed. The knees point upward.

 11 Then the sun

Sit up with an elongated back, arms in fifth position. The legs remain straight and the toes pointed, with the knees pointed upward.

 12 Begins to disappear.

Open the arms to second, then *allongé* and place the hands on the floor behind you.

 13 I feel a chill in the air.

Wrap the arms tightly around the shoulders and begin to twist from the waist right and left. Keep the legs in second position, stretched and toes pointed.

 14 I close my petals, to keep myself warm, as slowly as I can.

Begin to close the legs slowly with the legs straight and toes pointed. Once the legs are together, draw the knees to the chest tightly. Wrap the arms tightly around the knees with the head reaching down toward the knees.

 15 Now night time has come, it's time for me to rest. So I rock myself to sleep. Back and forth, back and forth, back and forth

Holding on to the position tightly, begin to rock back until the backs of the shoulders are on the floor, and come up again. Repeat this several times.

 16 Until I'm sleeping deep.

Stop rocking and assume the starting position of the exercise.

I'm a Butterfly

Goals

Warm up hips.

Increase hip flexibility.

Strengthen inner thighs.

Strengthen abdominals.

Increase flexibility and strength in the back.

Presentation and principles

Ask the class to think of their legs as butterfly wings.

Imitate butterfly wings in flight by bouncing the legs up and down in a gentle and controlled motion. Tell the students not to flap their wings too hard.

Press legs down to the ground to stop flying and achieve maximum flexibility.

Press elbows into knees to push the legs down while bending over to reach the flower. This will help increase each student's flexibility.

Slow the wings down by bringing knees together and rounding the back. This will work the inner thighs and abdominal muscles while stretching the upper back.

Pointing the feet while opening and closing the legs will reinforce the principle of pointing the feet throughout the duration of a movement.

Correcting common mistakes

Bounce knees gently.

Sit up tall while opening legs to second position.

Keep knees facing the ceiling while in second position.

Keep toes pointed when opening (to second position) and closing as a butterfly.

Advancement

This exercise should be repeated two times consecutively during every class to achieve maximum flexibility.

Switch to using the instrumental version of the music once the students know the exercise.

I'm A Butterfly

 1 Begin sitting up with an elongated back. The soles of the feet are together with the knees open and pressed down to the floor while holding the ankles with your hands.

 2 I'm a butterfly, watch me flutter by, as I spread my pretty wings and

Gently bounce the knees slightly up and down 16 times while still sitting tall.

 3 Fly

While still sitting tall open the legs and arms to second position.

On the 4 counts of music after the word **fly**, close the legs again to the starting position, with the soles of the feet together.

 4 Flutter and I fly, flutter and I fly, flutter and I fly, as you watch me flutter by

Repeat 2 through 4.

 5 Now I'm getting

Pull the knees up and together rounding the back.

 6 Tired

Open the knees again pressing them down to the floor with the back elongated.

 7 My wings are slowing down, better find a flower, way down on the...

Repeat 5 and 6 three more times.

 8 Ground.

Round over, reaching the head to the feet with the knees opened and pressing down to the floor.

 9 Hmmm

Sit up again with an elongated back, to the starting position.

 10 Hmmm...

Holding on to the ankles with the knees still opened, rock to the right trying to hold the back elongated.

11 ...it smells so good

Repeat the rock to the left.

 12 Hmmm, I like this little flower, hmmm I'd like to stay an hour, but it's time for me to flutter, cause I've got to find another.

Rock right and left 4 more times.

Sit up with an elongated back to the starting position, and repeat the entire exercise.

Mr. Inchworm
Variations 1 and 2

Goals

Variation 1

Warm up and articulate feet.

Strenthen torso.

Warm up inner thighs and hamstrings.

Stretch hamstrings.

Achieve *développé*.

Variation 2

Hamstring and Achilles stretch.

Increase back flexibility.

Stretch entire front of the body.

Presentation and principles

Variation 1

Ask students to make their feet move like worms. This achieves a maximum articulation of the feet. When pointing, teach them to stretch through the ball of the foot before reaching through the toes. When flexing, teach them to flex the toes first and the ankle second. Since these actions take a lot of coordination, it will take some time for students to achieve fully–articulate pointed and flexed feet.

Roll down to the floor very, very slowly. This helps to develop maximum control of the abdominal muscles.

The foot should stay pointed throughout the *développé*. At the very top of the movement the foot may flex to achieve an intense stretch of the hamstrings. During the *développé*, the action of holding the thighs tightly together activates the inner thigh muscles. The hamstrings help to lift the leg. The quads hold their legs up in the air.

Sit up tall while rolling up from the floor. This strengthens the abdominal muscles and back.

Variation 2

In this variation, the entire body is the inchworm:

While walking in and out with the feet or the arms, the entire body is being warmed up and strengthened. Keep legs as straight as possible while walking to stretch hamstrings, lower back, and Achilles tendon.

When trying to poke your head up out of the ground, lift and push up with an elongated back to strengthen arms and back. Simultaneously rotate the shoulders down and lift the head to achieve an elongation of the neck.

Reaching the feet to the head achieves flexibility in both the front and the back of the body. Lifting the feet to the head also activates and strengthens the hamstrings.

Correcting common mistakes

Variation 1

Always sit up tall to elongate the back while flexing and pointing the feet.

Keep legs straight and toes pointed while rolling down to the floor.

Continually point toes during *développé*.

Squeeze upper thighs together during *développé*.

Straighten the leg and reach the toe up to the ceiling at the height of *développé*.

Keep legs straight and toes pointed while rolling up to sitting.

Variation 2

Keep legs as straight as possible while walking up and down.

Press shoulders down while lifting torso off the ground.

Push down to straighten arms while touching toes to head.

Advancement

Begin with the first variation and repeat it twice. Then advance to the second variation, executing it only one time. The second variation may be repeated twice once the students are able to do the exercise with proper technique.

Once they become strong enough, cut the amount of time each action takes. Take eight counts instead of taking sixteen to walk up and down. (They will then be going up and down twice within the sixteen counts.)

Alternate the variations week to week, only doing one within a class.

Mr. Inchworm

Variation 1

 1 Begin sitting up with an elongated back. The legs are outstretched in front of you with the legs very straight and the toes pointed.

 2 Mr. Inchworm crawls beneath the ground, down where it's dark and cool. See his wiggly body go up and down

Flex and point the feet seven times while keeping the back elongated.

 3 Very, very, slowly,

Begin to roll down slowly, with your back rounding over and the chin to the chest, until you are lying flat on the floor. The legs stay straight with the toes pointed throughout.

 4 Inch by inch he crawls.

Keeping the legs tightly together draw the right leg up slowly until the right foot is on the left ankle in *coupé*, while keeping the toes pointed.

 5 Making a tunnel to the top of the ground

Continue to draw the right leg up until the right foot is on the left knee in *passé*. Keep the legs pulled tightly together and the toes pointed throughout.

 6 Sticks up his head

Slowly *développé* the leg, extending it to the ceiling, until the leg is straight. Keep the toes pointed throughout.

 7 But then he frowns.

Flex the right foot, while keeping the leg straight.

 8 It's too bright.

Point the right foot again, while keeping the leg straight.

 9 I'm going back.

Bring the right foot back to the left knee to the *passé* position. Keep the legs together tightly with the toes pointed.

10 Down.

Slide the right foot down the left leg and extend it until it is straight. Keep the legs tightly together with the toes pointed.

 11

On the next two counts of the music, roll up off the floor, beginning with the head. Bring the chin to the chest and lift each vertebra off the floor, until you are sitting up in the starting position. Keep the legs straight and the toes pointed throughout.

Repeat the entire exercise using the left leg.

Mr. Inchworm

Variation 2

 1 Begin in a large circle, lying down, with heads down and pointing into the circle. Place hands next to shoulders with the palms on the floor. The elbows should be tucked tightly to the body.

 2 Mr. Inchworm crawls beneath the ground. Down where it's dark and cool.

Begin walking the feet inward toward the hands, trying to keep the legs as straight as possible, until you walk the feet as close to the hands as possible. Try to keep legs straight. This should take sixteen counts with the music, taking sixteen small steps.

 3 See his wiggly body go up and down. Very, very slowly.

Begin to walk the hands forward away from the feet, trying to keep the legs as straight as possible, until you are lying flat on the floor again in the starting position. This should take sixteen counts with the music, taking sixteen small steps. The circle will become smaller with the students closer together.

 4 Inch by inch he crawls, making a tunnel to the top of the ground. Sticks his head up.

Begin to push the hands on the floor to lift the upper body. Keep the legs straight and the toes pointed. Continue pushing until you can't go any further, keeping the hips on the ground. Then push against the floor, straightening the arms, lifting the head back and up. Try to keep the shoulders down, and again the legs remain straight, with the toes pointed.

 5 But then he frowns. It's too bright, I'm going back

Pick the feet up as you arch the back, reaching the head to the feet.

 6 Down.

Lie down on the floor, back to the starting position.

 7 Mr. Inchworm crawls beneath the ground, down where it's dark and cool.

Begin to walk the hands back towards the feet, trying to keep the legs as straight as possible, until your hands are close to the feet. This should take sixteen counts with the music, taking sixteen small steps.

8 See his wiggly body go up and down. Very, very, slowly.

Begin to walk the feet back, trying to keep the legs as straight as possible, until you are laying down on the floor, back in the starting position. This should take sixteen counts with the music, taking sixteen small steps. The circle is now back to its original position.

 9 Inch by inch he crawls. Making a tunnel to the top of the ground.

Begin pushing the hands against the floor to lift the chest off of the floor. Keep the legs straight and the toes pointed.

 10 Sticks up his head.

Lift the head up straightening the arms. Try to push the shoulders down as the head goes up.

 11 But then he frowns: it's too bright, I'm going back

Bring the feet up and the head back to touch each other, while keeping the toes pointed.

 12 Down.

Lie down on the floor again, back to the starting position.

Repeat the entire exercise.

I'm A Big Oak Tree

Goals

Warm up and strengthen legs, ankles and feet.

Stretch hamstrings.

Articulate arm movements.

Successfully follow turning directions, right and left.

Create proper circular spatial directions, right and left.

Achieve balance.

Increase aerobic activity.

Presentation and principles

To imitate a growing tree, first straighten the legs while keeping hands on the floor. This achieves maximum hamstring stretch.

The students are learning to balance while stretching from the waist in second position. It will help them to keep straight, pulled up legs throughout the movement.

Begin moving elbows upward and downward to achieve a soft movement of the arms when imitating the movements of a bird's wings.

Running on the toes will teach students what it is to *bourrée*. It also strengthens their feet and ankles.

Specify turning and circular spatial directions to teach right and left.

Have your students follow one another while keeping the circle.

Correcting common mistakes

Keep hands on the floor while straightening legs.

Keep legs very straight and pulled up while opening to parallel second position.

Reach hands down to the sides of legs for maximum stretch when stretching torso.

Bend elbows to fly like a bird.

Give reminders constantly about which is right and which is left.

Keep the circle by following one another.

Advancement

This exercise should be executed in every class. There are many movements within this exercise that will take time to develop.

Change the turning and running directions from class to class.

Use the instrumental version of the music once the students know the exercise.

I'm A Big Oak Tree

 1 Form a circle. Begin in a squatting position, with the hands on the floor in front of you.

 2 I'm a big oak tree,

Straighten the legs as much as possible with the hands still on the floor.

 3 Growing up so high.

Continue to a standing position, with the arms reaching up overhead.

 4 Spreading out my branches, reaching for the sky.

Open the legs to a wide parallel second position. The arms reach up and out diagonally.

 5 When the breeze begins to blow, it sways me to and fro. Whistling through my branches, back and forth I go.

Bend sideways from the waist right and left, while the legs remain straight, with the arms overhead.

 6 All the pretty birds, soaring in the sky, round and round they go.

Begin to run (*bourrée*) on the toes, while flapping the arms like the wings of a bird.

 7 Round and round they fly.

Continue the *bourrées* turning in place right or left.

 8 They use my pretty leaves to hide behind—my branches are their home—they fly and fly, and circle round and find a branch,

Continue running (*bourrée*) on the toes in a big circle right or left. The arms continue flapping.

 9 And all sit down.

Find your starting spot and squat down again to the starting position of the exercise.

Repeat the entire exercise once.

Coupé the Cricket

Goals

Introduce barre work.

Learn the terminology for and basic mechanics of *coupé*.

Learn the terminology for and basic mechanics of *passé*.

Transition from *coupé* to *passé*.

Achieve balance.

Strengthen inner thighs and hamstrings.

Achieve proper shaping of the foot when pointed in the air.

Improve musicality.

Presentation and principles

Students this age imitate older students standing at the barre, so they enjoy doing this exercise. They learn how to do their preparation at the barre as well as how to finish an exercise at the barre.

Using the imagery of a cricket rubbing its legs together to make its sounds will teach the students to slide the working leg up and down the standing leg tightly.

Working in the parallel position (keeping the thighs together) will help to avoid a sickled foot and shape the pointed foot correctly.

The repetition of the *coupé* and *passé* in the lyrics helps them to remember the terminology for the positions.

The students learn how to use the barre, holding on lightly while trying to balance on their own.

Have the students move their legs at different speeds with the music to teach varied rhythms.

Common Mistakes and Corrections:

Hold legs tightly together throughout the exercise.

Point the foot when it leaves the floor.

Take the *passé* leg up high (to the knee), standing up tall throughout the exercise.

No leaning on the barre!

Advancement

Although not shown here, this exercise can also be done while sitting or lying on the floor.

To begin to work more intensely on their balance, have the students hold their arms in first position when doing the first sixteen counts of the song and the barre on the faster movements.

This is a valuable exercise since it reinforces the *coupé* and *passé* positions that the children will be using for much of their center floor work. It should be executed in every class, and can be modified during each class for variety. Sitting, lying on the floor and standing are all appropriate options.

Coupé the Cricket

 1 Begin facing the barre with the arms down (*en bas*). The feet are in first position parallel.

 2 Prepare for movement while the introduction music plays. Arms come to first position, then are placed on the barre.

 3 Coupé

Bend the right knee bringing the right foot tightly to the ankle of the left leg, with the toes pointed (*coupé*).

 4 the Cricket

Slide the right leg up to the knee of the left leg (to *passé*), keeping the toes pointed and the legs held tightly together.

 5 Sings his pretty

Slide the right leg back down to the ankle (*coupé*).

 6 Song.

Bring the feet back together, with the legs straight to parallel first position.

 7 Coupé

Repeat the *coupé* position with the right foot.

 8 the Cricket,

Repeat the *passé* position with the right foot.

 9 Won't you sing

Bring the foot back to the *coupé* position.

 10 Along?

Then back to the starting position, parallel first.

 11 *Coupé, passé, coupé,* first.
Coupé, passé, coupé, first.

Execute the positions with the lyrics. This will be faster than when done previously. Repeat two times.

12 He rubs his legs together and says chirp, chirp, chirp!

Remain with the feet together in parallel first on the lyrics. After the lyrics you will hear three beats of music. Slide the right leg up and down from *coupé* to *passé* quickly three times. The last movement will finish feet together in parallel first. The leg accents downward on the 3 beats.

The lyrics will repeat from the beginning. Repeat the entire exercise with the left leg.

Finish with the arms down (*en bas*).

Center Floor Exercises
Tendu the Tulip
Variations 1 and 2

Goals

Variation 1

Learn the terminology for and basic mechanics of *tendu* front, *développé, coupé, passé, relevé,* and *bourrée* turns.

Successfully follow directions in turns (right and left).

Successfully shift weight quickly.

Achieve balance.

Achieve fifth position of the arms.

Properly end the exercise.

Variation 2

Properly work in a slightly open-toed position.

Achieve *tendu* side and *temps lié.*

Achieve proper leg alignment in an open position.

Presentation and principles

Variation 1

Exaggerate movements while demonstrating the proper execution of *développé* and *enveloppé.*

The lyrics of the song help students remember what a *tendu* is and reinforces right and left directions.

When first introducing this exercise, it is sufficient for the students to know to pick the foot up and place it on the floor. They tend to automatically respond with a pointed foot.

The students are learning how to make a quick change of weight while maintaining balance when doing spring points (jumping from one foot to the other).

The students are learning *passé* and how to balance on one leg when they step and point side.

Work on *bourrée* turns to reinforce directional turning and to give the students full use of their feet and ankles in *relevé.*

Reinforce the proper ending to a center floor exercise by opening from fifth position to second position and finishing with the arms down (*en bas*).

Variation 2

In this variation, adding an open-toed position will begin to teach students correct alignment of the legs. Turnout should be minimal.

Knees should be over the toes when doing a *plié* and the heel of the moving leg should be forward when doing a *tendu* side.

This exercise is the student's first introduction to *temps lié* and second position *plié*.

Introduce the concept of sliding the foot out to *tendu* position.

Correcting common mistakes

Variation 1

Keep toes pointed while executing the spring points.

Stand tall to achieve balance.

Touch toe to knee in *passé*.

Go high in *relevé* on the *bourrée* turns (way up on the toes for the tip–toe dance).

Variation 2

Keep knees over toes during every *plié*.

Keep leg straight and heel forward when sliding into and out of *tendu*.

Distribute weight evenly on both legs during *temps lié*.

You may find that when first introducing this exercise the students have a tendency to sickle their feet. This will improve with repetition of working in the parallel position during floor exercises. This exercise will specifically help students to use their feet properly. Keep in mind this will take time to develop.

Advancement

Once the students have learned the basic concepts of the movements, you can work on being more exact. Start to tighten their *coupé* positions on the *développés* and *enveloppés*. You should not try to enforce this until they have mastered the Coupé the Cricket exercise.

This exercise should be executed in every class. There is much to be accomplished in the first variation before advancing to the second. Be sure not to advance to the second variation too soon.

Once the students have mastered the concept of using the right foot first, use the instrumental version of the music and teach the exercise using the left foot first for both variations. The turns should also go to the left.

Once the students have mastered balance, begin to add *port de bras*. For instance, bring the arms to fifth position on the *passé*.

Tendu the Tulip

Variation 1

 1 Begin with the feet together and hands on hips.

 2 I'm Tendu

Bend the right knee and pick up the right foot with the toes pointed. Extend the right foot to *tendu* front (*développé*) with the standing leg bent (*plié*).

 3 the Tulip

Bend the right knee again to pick up the right foot, with the toes pointed (*enveloppé*), and place the feet back together again with the legs straight.

 4 I *tendu* right and left.

Bend the right knee again picking up the right foot and *développé* to *tendu* front. Jump, changing the feet to *tendu* front left, then bring the feet back together.

 5 I'm Tendu the Tulip—I *tendu* right and left.

Repeat steps 2 through 4.

 6 I step to the right and point

Step with the right foot to the side. Pick up the left foot to the right knee (*passé*), with the right leg straight. *Développé* the left foot to *tendu* front, with the right leg in *plié*.

 7 I step to the left and point

Repeat the step and point to the left.

 8 Doing my tip–toe dance in my garden

Press up on to the toes (*relevé*), with the arms in fifth position and turn to the right taking tiny steps with the feet together (*bourrée* turn), until you have completed one full turn. Finish facing front again.

9 All day long.

With the feet together come down with the knees bent (*plié*), bringing the hands back to the hips.

10 I'm Tendu the Tulip, I *tendu* right and left.

Repeat 2 through 4 again.

11

For the next 8 counts of music, bend (*plié*) and straighten the knees four times.

Repeat the exercise from the beginning.

To finish, open the arms side (second position) and bring them down (*en bas*).

Tendu the Tulip

Variation 2

 1 Begin with heels together and the toes open slightly (first position), with the hands on the hips and the legs straight.

 2 I'm Tendu the Tulip

Extend the right foot to the side, with the leg straight and the toes pointed. The inside of the heel should be facing front (*tendu*). Then close the right leg again to the starting position.

 3 I *tendu* right

Point the right foot side again (*tendu*).

 4 And

Place the weight on both legs evenly with the knees bent (second position *plié*).

5 Left.

Straighten the legs again, with all of the weight on the right leg.
The toes of the left foot are pointed.
(The combined movements in figures 4 and 5 are called a *temps lié*).

 6

Bring the left foot back in again to the starting position.

 7 I'm Tendu the Tulip I *tendu* right and left.

Repeat figures 2 through 6.

 8 I step to the right,

Step the right foot side.

 9 And

Pick up the left foot to the right knee, with the toes pointed, to *passé* parallel.

10 Point.

Straighten the left leg reaching it front, with the toes pointed (*tendu*), while the right leg is bent (in *plié*).

11 I step to the left and point.

Repeat 8, 9 and 10 to the left side.

**12 Doing my tip–toe dance,
in my garden,**

Come up onto the toes (*relevé*), with the arms in fifth position. Taking tiny steps with the feet together (*bourrée*), turn to the right.

13 All day long.

Come down from the *relevé* with the feet together, back to the starting position, with the hands on the hips.

**14 I'm Tendu the Tulip,
I *tendu* right and left.**

Repeat figures 2 through 6
one more time.

15

Bend both knees (*plié*).

16

Straighten the legs.

Repeat 15 and 16, bending and straightening the knees four more times with the remainder of the music.

Port de bras the Spider

Goals

Achieve fifth position of the arms.

Grasp the concept of *port de bras*.

Move arms with fluidity.

Differentiate between high positions of the arms (*en haut*) and the low positions of the arms (*demi-bras*).

Presentation and principles

The lyrics of this song help the students learn the five basic positions of the arms quickly.

Point out that there are low positions and high positions when moving through the different third positions.

Let the students take turns being the teacher, having them stand in front while the other students follow them.

Correcting common mistakes

Students at this age have a tendency to lock their arms. Work on trying to keep the elbows softened.

When using the high positions (*en haut*), remind students to keep their shoulders down.

Advancement

Once the students master leading with the right arm, begin using the left.

Once they are comfortable with the exercise, you can begin to teach them how to use their heads by following the moving arm and inclining the head towards the leading arm.

Port de bras the Spider

 1 Begin feet together in parallel first, with the arms down (*en bas*).

 2 Port de bras   Sway the arms right to middle third position.

 3 the Spider   Sway the arms left to middle third position.

 4 Has so many arms.   Repeat 2 and 3.

 5 She moves them   Sway the arms overhead right to high third position.

 6 Oh so gracefully   Sway the arms overhead left to high third position.

 7 She'll win you with her charms.   Repeat 5 and 6.

 8 Port de bras   Sway the arms right again to middle third.

 9 the Spider   Sway the arms left again to middle third.

 10 Counts her arms   Sway the arms right again to middle third.

 11 Of eight.   Bring the arms down (*en bas*).

12 One   Bring the right arm up in front of you to first position.

	13 Two	Bring the left arm up to first position.
	14 Three	Open the right arm to the side to second position.
	15 Four	Open the left arm to second position.
	16 Five	Bring the right arm overhead to fifth position.
	17 Six	Bring the left arm to fifth position.
	18 Seven	Bring the right arm back down to first position.
	19 And	Bring the left arm to first position.
	20 Eight	Bring both arms down *en bas*.
	21 She can bring her arms to first	Bring both arms to first position.
	22 And second	Bring both arms to second position.
	23 Third	Bring the right arm overhead to third position.
	24 And fourth	Bring the left arm front to fourth position.
	25 And fifth	Bring the left arm overhead to fifth position.
	26 Then opens them up	Open both arms to second position.

27 And they

Stretch the arms with palms down to second position *allongé*.

28 Float down.

Bring both arms down *en bas*.

29 Then *port de bras*

Bring both arms front through first position then overhead to fifth position.

30 All

Open both arms side to second position.

31 Around.

Open both arms side to second position, then stretch the arms palms down to *allongé* and down *en bas*.

32

Repeat figures 2 through 32 to the right or left. For the remaining eight counts of the music bend the knees (*demi–plié*) and straighten the legs four times with the music.

Skippy the Squirrel
Variation 1, Front and back
Variation 2, Right and left

Goals

Learn spatial directions (front, back, right, left).

Differentiate between directions while turning.

Successfully skip forward, backward and sideways.

Successfully hold arms in the desired shape while executing a movement.

Change the body shape while executing a movement.

End in the desired pose.

Improve musicality.

Strengthen abdominals and thighs.

Learn to dance in a specific pattern as a group.

Presentation and principles

This exercise works on refining and developing the basic motor skill called skipping.

The students will learn to move through space in forward, backward, right and left directions. They will also learn to turn in a desired direction, right or left, while skipping.

We do this exercise as a group, dancing in a single line, horizontally and vertically in the room. The students learn how to work together to keep the desired spatial design.

The action of scooping up nuts brings their arms to first position and changes the body shape to a rounded back. They explore skipping while holding the body in a different shape and keeping the arms in first position.

Students learn to concentrate and improve their musicality by bouncing in time to the music to start and end the exercise.

We stop skipping because we see a nut on the ground. When this happens, the students are asked to stop in a certain pose. One way to stop is with feet together and arms up and back. You can vary the poses or have the students invent their own poses.

When descending to and rising from the floor in the crossed–leg position, the students will develop leg and abdominal strength.

Correcting common mistakes

Keep feet pointed and hold a tight *passé* position while skipping.

Hold the rounded back position while skipping and keep the arms in first position.

Freeze and be absolutely still when posing.

Keep hands off the floor when going into and out of the crossed leg position.

Hold spatial patterns throughout entire exercise.

Advancement

Once the students understand the front and back spatial directions, begin to work on skipping backwards when moving to the back. When doing the right and left version the students can work on skipping sideways, right and left.

You can vary the poses to make them more challenging. Change from a standing position to a squatting position.

Skippy the Squirrel

Variation 1, Front and back

 1 Begin with feet together, the hands on the hips.

 2 Busy Skippy Squirrel works hard in the garden all day, gathering nuts for winter, he has no time to play.

Bend the knees (*demi–plié*), then straighten the legs. Repeat this eight times bouncing up and down with the music.

 3 He skips to the front

With the hands on hips, skip, moving forward to the front of the room.

 4 Because he sees a nut.

Stop with the feet together and the arms up, while looking down on the ground.

 5 He picks it up

Bend over and reach to the floor.

 6 And skips around

Stand up with the arms in first position.

 7 To find another nut.

Skip around, turning right, to face the back. Finish feet together, with the arms in first position.

 8 He skips to the back

Skip forward again to the back of the room.

 9 To find another nut.

Stop with the feet together with arms up.

 10 He picks it up

Bend over reaching to the ground.

11 And skips around

Stand up with the arms in first position.

12 To find another nut

Skip around to the right to face the front again with the arms in first position. Finish with the feet together.

 13 These nuts are getting heavy.

Bend the knees (*demi-plié*) and bend over slightly from the waist.

 14 I'll go back to my nest

Skip forward, still bent over slightly, moving forward. Finish in the center of the room where you started and stop with the feet together.

 15 And put them in my hiding place,

Bend down reaching the arms to the floor while keeping them in first position.

 16 Sit down and

Stand up and cross the right foot behind the left with the arms out and to the sides (second position *allongé*).

 17 Take a rest

Keeping the feet crossed, sit down, placing the hands under the chin with the elbows leaning on the legs. Remain in this position for four counts of the music.

 18

Come up to a standing position, on the next four counts of the music, with the feet together and the hands on the hips. Back to the starting position.

Repeat the entire exercise once more.

Skippy the Squirrel

Variation 2, Right and left

All of the movements to the lyrics are the same as in the previous exercise. In this version, we have changed the spatial design to a vertical line and we skip to the right and left of the room.

Chassé the Chipmunk
Variation 1, One clap
Variation 2, Two claps
Variation 3, Three claps

Goals

One clap and two claps

Learn the terminology for and basic mechanics of *chassé*.

Correctly follow spatial directions (right, left and circling).

Improve musicality and rhythm.

Strengthen feet and ankles.

Increase aerobic activity.

Three claps

Learn to work with a partner.

Correctly follow more intricate spatial directions.

Achieve balance.

Presentation and principles

One clap and two claps

Since this exercise has many variations, you may vary them from class to class.

In this exercise the students work on a basic motor skill, galloping, that is called *chassé* in ballet terminology. The lyrics of the song will help students to remember this term.

The students work on their musicality and rhythm by learning how to execute different clapping rhythms with the music.

The imagery of reaching up in the tall grass ensures a full use of the *relevé* position and strengthens both feet and ankles.

The position used before the *relevé* teaches the student to *plié* before *relevé*.

The constant movement of the arms up and down while clapping makes this exercise an excellent aerobic activity.

The students work on forming multiple spatial designs. They dance in a line while creating circular movements.

Three claps

The students work on balance and musicality by clapping three times in *relevé*.

The students learn to work with a partner while executing the circular spatial design.

The students learn how to work in opposition, maintaining the right and left spacial directions. Partners are facing each other. They learn that when they both go to the right, they are moving in the opposite direction.

Correcting common mistakes

One clap and two claps

Work on refining the *chassé*, asking the students to jump higher. This will in turn make them use their feet, pointing their toes to push off of the floor. For further refinement of the *chassé*, explain to the students that *chassé* means "to chase." One leg chases the other so that the legs come together in the air.

Encourage students to reach as high as they can on the claps for the maximum *relevé* position.

The number of *chassés* will change from one clap to two claps. One clap has four *chassés* and two claps have three *chassés*. The correct sequence can be achieved in time with repetition.

Three claps

It will take some time for the students to understand that no matter where they are facing the right and left directions do not change.

Advancement

One clap and two claps

The music for this exercise is repeated, once with lyrics and once without. You can change the starting directions and circular movements (beginning with the left on the second verse) so that they begin to learn how to reverse the movements and directions.

Three claps

Have the students trade places with their partners. This will further their understanding of the right and left directions.

Chassé the Chipmunk

Variation 1, One clap

 1 Begin with feet together, hands on the hips.

 2 Oh where is Chassé Chipmunk, in the tall grass

Bend (*demi–plié*) and straighten the knees four times, bouncing with the music.

 3 He knows that I can't find him so

Step to the right with the right leg as you bend the knees (*plié*). Then bring the left leg to the right leg, while jumping and straightening the knees. This is a galloping step, done sideways (the ballet terminology is *chassé*). Do this four times moving to the right.

 4 He reaches up and

Finish with the feet together and the knees bent (*plié*). The arms are reaching out to the sides with the palms facing up.

 5 Claps.

Straighten the legs with the feet still together. Push all the way up on the toes (*relevé*), as you reach the arms straight up overhead and clap once.

 6 Oh where is Chassé Chipmunk, in the tall grass. He knows that I can't find him, so he reaches up and claps.

Repeat movements 2 through 5, this time moving to the left.

 7 He *chassés* all around, through the pretty

Chassé to the right six times, making your own circle right. End facing front again.

 8 Flowers.

Do one more *chassé* but finish by jumping the feet together, hands on the hips, facing front. The knees are bent (*plié*).

9 Have you found him yet?

Open the arms side with the palms facing up with the knees bent (*plié*).

 10

On the next three counts of the music, reach up with the legs straight and still together. Push up to the toes (*relevé*) while reaching the arms straight up overhead and clap three times.

Repeat the entire exercise, 2 through 10. This repeat has no lyrics.

At the end of the exercise bend (*plié*) and straighten the knees four times, bouncing with the music (as done in movements 2 and 3).

Chassé the Chipmunk

Variation 2, Two claps

 1 Begin with feet together, hands on the hips.

 2 Oh where is Chassé Chipmunk, in the tall grass?

Bend (*demi-plié*) and straighten the knees four times, bouncing with the music.

 3 He *chassés* to the right.

Step to the right with the right leg as you bend the knees (*plié*). Then bring the left leg to the right leg, while jumping and straightening the knees. This is a galloping step, done sideways (the ballet terminology is *chassé*). Do this three times moving to the right. On the third one, finish with the feet together with the knees bent (*plié*) and the arms reaching out to the sides, palms facing up.

 4

You will hear two claps with the music. Clap two times over head with the feet together reaching up on to the toes (*relevé*). Come down in between the claps with the knees bent (*plié*) and the arms reaching out to the sides, palms facing up.

 5 Oh where is Chassé Chipmunk in the tall grass? He *chassés* to the left (clap, clap).

Repeat 2 through 4, moving to the left.

 6 He *chassés* all around, through the pretty flowers.

Do the galloping step (*chassé*) eight times around in a circle, turning to the right.

7 Have you found him yet?

Jump with feet together, knees bent (*plié*) with arms reaching out to the sides, palms up.

 8

Clap three times overhead. The feet are together up on the toes (*relevé*).

 9

Repeat the entire exercise, 2 through 10. This repeat has no lyrics.

 10

At the end of the exercise bend (*plié*) and straighten the knees four times, bouncing with the music as done in figures 1 and 2.

Chassé the Chipmunk

Variation 3, Three claps

 1 Begin with feet together, hands on hips, facing your partner.

 2 I found him, I found him, in the tall grass.

Bend (*plié*) and straighten the knees two times.

 3 We *chassé* to the right.

Step to the right with the right leg as you bend the knees (*plié*). Then bring the left leg to the right leg, while jumping and straightening the knees. This is a galloping step, done sideways (the ballet terminology is *chassé*). Do this two times moving to the right. On the second one finish with the feet together, the knees bent (*plié*), and the arms reaching out to the sides, palms facing up.

Clap overhead three times. The feet are together up on the toes (*relevé*).

 4 I found him, I found him, in the tall grass.

Repeat 2.

 5 We *chassé* to the left (clap, clap, clap).

Repeat 2 and 3, doing the galloping step (*chassé*) to the left. This time you finish facing your partner, back where you started.

 6 We chassé all around, through the pretty flowers.

Take your partner's hands and *chassé* around with each other eight times, until you are back where you started.

 7 Did you find us yet (clap, clap, clap).

Finish with feet together and knees bent (*plié*). Arms are reaching out to the sides, palms up. Then clap overhead again three times with the feet together and up on the toes (*relevé*).

Repeat the entire exercise 2 through 7. This repeat has no lyrics. At the end of the exercise bend (*plié*) and straighten the knees four times, bouncing with the music, as done in 1 and 2.

Échappé Azalea

Goals

Learn the terminology for and basic mechanics of *échappé*.

Strengthen legs, ankles, and feet.

Increase aerobic activity.

Point the toes when leaving the floor.

Use *plié* to gain momentum for a jump.

Improve musicality.

Presentation and principles

The song lyrics help students remember the terminology and movements of an *échappé*.

The bouncing (*plié*) used in this exercise enforces the use of *plié* before jump.

Bouncing and jumping with different rhythms develops the student's musicality.

At the beginning of the exercise, the jumps are spaced apart. As the exercise progresses, the jumps are closer together. Jumping in time with the music will help to develop the student's musicality.

Students learn to gain momentum for their jumps through use of the double bounce (*plié*). As the students try to jump higher they are more apt to use their feet, pointing them for the jump.

Correcting common mistakes

Jump up, before opening or closing the legs, to gain maximum elevation.

Jump higher to use feet and instinctively point.

Keep back straight and stand tall while bouncing.

Advancement

Switch to using the instrumental version of the music once the students know the exercise.

The *échappé* can also be done in fourth position. Open the legs with one foot in front of the other. Alternate the feet, opening with the right and then the left foot in front.

Échappé Azalea

 1 Begin feet together in first position with the hands on the hips.

 2 I'm Échappé

Bend the knees (*plié*) as far as you can with the heels remaining on the floor.

 3

Then straighten the knees.

 4 Azalea.

Repeat 2 and 3.

 5 I bounce

Bent the knees (*plié*) slightly.

 6 And

Come back to straight knees.

 7 Bounce

Bend the knees (*plié*) as far as you can with heels remaining on the floor.

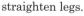 **8 And jump.**

Jump up in the air with feet together in first position. Then open legs to second position, while still in the air. Land in second position with knees bent (*plié*).

9

Remain in second position and straighten legs.

 10 I'm Échappé

Bend (*plié*) and straighten knees.

 11 Azalea.

Repeat 10.

 12 I bounce

Bend the knees (*plié*) slightly.

13 And   Come back to straight knees.

14 Bounce   Bend the knees (*plié*) as far as you can
                                with heels remaining on the floor.

15 And jump.   Jump up in the air with legs open in
                                second position. While still in the air,
                                close the legs together to first position.
                                Land feet together with the knees bent
                                (*plié*) in first position.

16   Keeping the legs together in first position,
                                straighten the knees.

**17 Bounce and bounce jump out   Repeat 5 through 8.
to second.**

**18 Bounce and bounce jump in   Repeat 12 through 15.
to first.**

19 Out, in, out, in, out, in. Jump out to second then into first
                                three times.

20   Finish with legs together in first position,
                                legs straight.

                                Repeat the entire exercise.

Bourrée the Bee

Goals

To learn the terminology for and basic mechanics of *bourrée*.

Strengthen ankles and feet.

Strengthen the *relevé* position.

Explore spatial directions and designs.

Learn *port de bras* of the body.

Stretch hamstrings.

Strengthen back.

Learn how to dance together as a group.

Spark creativity.

Presentation and principles

The song lyrics help students remember the terminology and movements of a *bourrée*.

Run in a high tip-toe to strengthen ankles and feet.

We have executed this exercise moving on the diagonals within the room. There are many different spatial designs and directions to explore. The exercise can be done in a straight line moving right and left or in a circle moving right and left. The spatial patterns can change when the music becomes instrumental.

When the students bend over from the hips, they are learning the *port de bras*. This position helps to strengthen their backs and stretch their hamstrings. They have fun with this movement, making a slurping sound while drinking the nectar.

I have shown this exercise as a group dance. It can be done with the students trading off the roles of leader and follower. It can also be practiced as an individual creative movement exercise. When working individually, students develop their ability to create their own spatial designs and directions.

Set the directions of the turns before beginning the exercise so the students may develop their spatial orientation and awareness of directions.

Be consistent with corrections on directional turning. Regularity will help the students' directional sense develop more rapidly.

Correcting common mistakes

Stand high on the toes during the *bourrée*.

Keep legs straight and back flat for maximum stretch and strengthening during the *port de bras*.

Advancement

There are endless possibilities for advancement in the creation of more intricate spatial designs.

You can do the exercise with more than one group working at the same time. This will teach the students to use their own space and to respect the space being used by their fellow dancers.

You can refine the *bourrée* by asking them to keep their feet in a tight first position.

Bourrée the Bee

 1 Begin in a circle facing each other with hands on hips and feet together in first position at one end of the room. Place flowers *(painted mats; see page 5)* **scattered around the room in desired positions.**

 2 Buzz, buzz, buzz, who makes that sound?

Push up to a high *relevé* and begin running on the toes, with very quick steps (*bourrée*). Pull the elbows in close to the body and flap the hands from the wrists to emulate a small bee's wings.

 3 Buzz, buzz, buzz, she *bourrées* all around.

Continue the *bourrées* as you turn right or left.

 4 She looks for a flower

Stop turning and face each other in the circle once again, looking down at the flower on the floor.

 5 Puts her head in for a bite,

Come down from the *relevé* with feet together in first position, keeping the legs straight. Bend over from the hips, while keeping the back flat (*port de bras* of the body). The arms reach straight out behind you.

 6 Then stands up again, and begins her next flight.

Come back up to a standing position. Begin the *bourrées* again, turning right or left, with the hands flapping.

 7 Buzz, buzz, buzz, she *bourrées* to the right. She finds a flower within her sight.

Bourrée to the right of the room on the diagonal, where the next flower is placed. Make a circle around the flower while looking down at it.

 8 She puts her head in, just for a bite,

Bend over once again from the hips with a flat back, to the *port de bras* position. The arms are reaching straight back.

**9 She stands up again,
and begins her next flight.**

Come back up to a standing position. Begin the *bourrées* again, turning right or left, with the hands flapping.

 **10 Buzz, buzz, buzz,
she *bourrées* to the left.**

Bourrée on the diagonal to the next flower, which is placed on the left side of the room.

 **11 She drinks all the nectar
till there's nothing left. She puts
her head in, just for a bite.**

Make a circle around the flower while looking down at it. Bend over once again from the hips with a flat back, to the *port de bras* position. The arms are reaching straight back.

 **12 She stands up again, and begins
her next flight.**

Come back up to a standing position. Begin the *bourrées* again, turning right or left, with the hands flapping.

This exercise repeats from the beginning with no lyrics.

Sauté the Bunny

Goals

Refine basic motor skills (hopping and jumping).

Improve musicality (rhythm comprehension).

Learn the decorum of a dance class when working across the floor.

Strengthen legs, ankles and feet.

Achieve balance.

Learn the terminology for and basic mechanics of *sauté* and *assemblé*.

Successfully follow spatial directions.

Presentation and principles

The song lyrics help the students remember the terminology and movements of a *sauté*.

Timing for the hops and the jumps is coordinated with the music to develop a sense of rhythm and musicality.

Students learn the decorum of dance class. They learn to wait for their group's turn when going across the floor.

Complete the phrase of two hops (either right or left) with an *assemblé*. This teaches students the basis of assembling their legs together in the air and landing in the appropriate position on two feet.

Work on developing their understanding of hopping on the same foot as the direction in which they are traveling.

The students develop a sense of balance while hopping on one leg.

Reinforce the spatial directions right and left.

The students learn to differentiate between a hop and a jump.

Correcting common mistakes

Work together and keep the formation through the entire exercise.

Watch the group that is dancing while waiting your turn.

Jump high to point your toes.

Stretch tall to jump.

Keep back straight and tall when hopping to balance.

An assistant can be very helpful during this exercise. She or he can keep children focused and excited about waiting for their turn while the teacher helps those who are dancing.

Advancement

Further develop a sense of rhythm and musicality by using the instrumental music. The students will listen to the music as a cue for their hops and jumps rather than follow the vocal instruction in the lyrics.

The directions of the hops and jumps can be varied from class to class during the instrumental version of the music.

Refine the hops by having children hold the leg they are not standing on in a tight *passé* with a pointed foot.

Begin to have students focus on assembling their feet together in the air before landing.

Sauté the Bunny

1 Begin with feet together in first position with the hands on the hips. In this picture we are working in two groups, getting ready to go across the floor, standing on one side of the room. The first group is standing in front, and the second group is standing behind them.

2 Sauté the Bunny

Hold position 1.

3

You will hear 3 beats of music with a knocking sound after the word **"bunny."** On those beats, hop to the right, on the right foot, 2 times. Then jump the feet together, back to first position on the third beat.

4 Hops around all day.

You will hear three beats of music again, with a knocking sound, beginning on the word **"day."** Hop to the left on the left foot two times. Then jump the feet together back to first position on the third beat.

**5 Hopping in the garden
With his friends he plays.**

Again you will hear three knocking sounds. The first one after the word **"garden,"** the second on the word **"with,"** and the third on the word **"plays."**

On these beats, execute three jumps moving forward with the feet remaining together in first position.

The next verse is a repeat of the previous movements.

6 He can hop to his right.

Repeat 3 on the three knocking sounds after the word **"right."**

7 He can hop to his left.

Repeat 4 on the three knocking sounds after the word **"left."**

**8 Then he jumps on two feet.
That's what he likes the best.**

Repeat 5, jumping again three times. The first jump is after the word **"feet."** The second jump is on the word **"what"** and the third jump is on the word **"best."**

9 Won't you come and join me,

The first group turns around and calls the second group out to join them.

10 And hop around all day?

The second group runs out and stands behind the first group, as the first group turns around to face the front again.

**11 Frolic in the garden,
and be my friend and play.**

Group one and group two bend the knees (*plié*) and straighten them four times in time with the music.

Repeat the entire exercise from the beginning. Both groups execute the repeat together. At the end of the repeat the first group will be all the way across the floor and they are finished.

Repeat the entire exercise for the third time. The second group repeats the exercise one more time until they are all the way across the floor.

We have executed this with two groups. It can be done individually or in pairs, moving across the room.

Pas de chat the Pansy

Goals

Learn the terminology for and basic mechanics of *pas de chat*.

Balance in the *passé* position.

Learn the rhythm and accents of the *pas de chat*.

Improve coordination.

Strengthen legs and feet.

Presentation and principles

The song lyrics reinforce the use of the term *pas de chat*.

Slowly break the *pas de chat* down into three movements: *passé*, *passé*, first position. This will teach the proper execution of the *pas de chat* and allow the students to work on balance.

The students will learn balance and coordination by having to jump and quickly change weight from one foot to the other.

Reinforce the accent of the *pas de chat* by having them finish in the desired first position on the floor, landing on the beat.

Correcting common mistakes

Hold legs tightly together in *passé*.

Point toes throughout the jump.

Land in first position.

Change legs during the big jump.

Advancement

This exercise should be repeated in every class. It will take time for students to develop proper coordination for such a complex jump. Once the students have developed their coordination, use the instrumental version of the music and have them *pas de chat* all the way across the room. Don't use the entire story line.

Once the students understand the concept of using the correct leg when jumping right and left, change spatial directions. Have them *pas de chat* to both the right and the left within the song's duration.

Pas de chat the Pansy

 1 Begin feet together in first position, with hands on hips.

 2 There's a pansy, in the garden

Bend the knees (*plié*) then straighten knees two times with the music.

3 And her name is Pas de chat

Press up to the balls of the feet as high as you can (*relevé*). Take tiny steps while staying in the *relevé* with the feet together in first position (*bourreé*) turning to the right, until you have completed one full turn to face the front again. The arms are in fifth position overhead.

 4 Although she's very shy, she's my favorite of them all

Crouch down bending the knees (*plié*) turning the body away from the front of the room with the feet still together in first position, with the hands over the face as if to hide.

 5 When I'm peeking, through my window, sometimes I see her dance

Staying crouched, place the hand on the forehead over the eyes, as if looking for something around the room.

 6 When she thinks no one is looking she begins to leap and prance

Execute another *bourreé* turn to the right, completing one full turn to face front, with feet together in first position and hands on the hips.

 7 *Passé*

Bring the right foot up to the left knee with the foot pointed, holding the legs tightly together (*passé*).

 8 *Passé*

Step onto the right foot and execute the *passé* with the left leg.

 9 First

Place the left foot down, feet together in first position.

10 *Passé, passé*, **first**

Repeat 7 through 9 one more time.

 11 Jump,

 12 Jump, the

Bring the right leg to the *passé* position again, while the left knee is bent (*plié*). Jump into the air while lifting the left knee up as well. Then land on the right leg with the knee bent (*plié*), and the left leg in the *passé* position. Finish feet together in first position, with the knees bent (*plié*). Figures 11 through 14 are executed four times on these words:

 13 Pas de chat Pansy

 14 Dance.

"Jump"

"Jump"

"Pas"

"Dance"

Plié the Poppy

Goals

Strengthen legs and feet.

Use *plié* before each jump.

Learn to work on the diagonal across the room.

Learn how to work with a partner.

Reinforce the terminology and execution of a *plié*.

Improve musicality.

Presentation and principles

The song lyrics help the students remember *plié*.

Have children bounce (*plié* to straight legs) on the beat, to develop musicality.

The students will learn the difference between a small (*demi*) *plié* and a big (*grand*) *plié*. The *demi-plié* is the bouncing at the beginning of the exercise and the *grand plié* occurs when squatting before the big jump.

Jumping from the squatting position will strengthen legs and feet.

You will find that students enjoy working with their partners. Suggest that they take turns being leaders—have one student be leader while moving diagonally from the left to the right of the room; then alternate when they reverse and go diagonally from the right to left of the room.

Correcting common mistakes

Run on the toes.

Keep knees directly over toes while squatting.

Jump as high as possible to have pointed feet while in the air.

Respect each other by not pulling or tugging on each other's hands while running.

Advancement

Let students engage creatively by allowing them to execute big jumps and leaps of their choice.

Plié the Poppy

 1 Begin with feet together in first position, hands on hips. This exercise is done on the diagonal across the room with students working in pairs.

 2 Plié the Poppy jumps and pops all day.

Bend the knees (*plié*) and straighten the legs four times with the music as follows:

bend / straight	bend / straight	bend / straight		bend / straight
"Plié"	**"Poppy"**	**"jumps"**	**"pops"**	**"day"**

 3 She runs on her toes

The first student runs on her toes to the center of the room.

 4 And *pliés* very low

Squat down with hands on the floor in front and the head down.

 5 And pops up so high to play.

Jump up high with feet pointed, reaching the arms straight up overhead.

 6 She runs round the garden

Run on the toes around the room back to your partner.

 8 They run on their toes

Both students run to the center of the room while holding hands.

 9 And *plié* very low

Both students squat down with hands on the floor in front of them.

10 Then pop up and play again.

They both jump up with feet pointed and arms reaching straight up overhead. Partners hold hands again, and run to the opposite corner of the room to finish. The next group of students repeats this movement. This should then be done in reverse, working on the opposite diagonal of the room.

Creative Movement

The music for this exercise incorporates all of the melodies from all of the exercises in the class. There are no set instructions for this exercise; the students are free to dance their own steps. You can use a variety of games while they have fun being creative.

Separate students into two lines sitting on the floor and into designated groups. The first group gets up and begins to dance. When the music changes, ask them to go back to their places and sit down while the next group gets up to dance, and so forth. Done in this way, students develop sensitivity to the music, listening for the changes of melodies. They have learned to take direction and take turns. We end the exercise with everyone dancing together for the last song.

Révérence

Goals

Grasp the concept of *révérence*.

Learn to curtsey.

Understand and follow proper decorum of a dance class.

Successfully complete the *port de bras*.

Correctly tendu and *bourrée* (turn).

Follow spatial direction (right and left).

Presentation and principles

The purpose of this exercise is to teach the students how a dance class should end. The students thank their teacher for giving them the class, and thank their fellow students as well.

They learn how to present their arms during curtsey and *révérence* by moving them from first position to second.

This exercise contains repetition to reinforce the fundamentals of *tendu* and of *bourrée* turns.

Reinforce spatial directions by having the students give *révérence* to the right and curtsey to the left.

Correcting common mistakes

Technical corrections should be kept to a minimum during this exercise. Focus should be placed on saying goodbye.

Advancement

This exercise should be done at the end of each class. Always leave time for the *révérence* to reinforce the decorum of the dance class.

Use the instrumental version of the music to reverse the right and left spatial directions.

You can vary this exercise by having the students curtsey and *révérence* while facing each other. They could also perform the exercise individually as they prepare to leave the room.

Révérence

 1 Begin feet together in first position with the arms rounded and down (*en bas*).

 2 It's time for me to say goodbye

Bring the arms to first position.

 3 To Inchworm and

Open the right arm to second position.

 4 Bourrée

Open the left arm to second position.

 5, 6 the Bee.

Stretch the arms out with palms facing down (*allongé*). Bring the arms back down to the *en bas* position.

 7 It's time for me to say goodbye

Repeat 2.

 8 To

Repeat 3.

 9 My garden

Repeat 4.

 10 Of fantasy.

Repeat 5 and 6.

 11 Goodbye Chassé Chipmunk in the tall grass

Step with right leg to side right. Pick up the left foot with the knee lifted high. Place the left foot in front of the right, on the floor with the toes pointed, to *tendu* front. The right leg is bent (*plié*). This movement is called *révérence*.

12 It's been fun having you in my ballet class.

Step with left foot to side left. Place the right foot behind the left with the front of the toes on the floor. The left leg is bent (*plié*). This movement is called a curtsey.

13 Good-bye to my teacher and all of my friends.

Repeat 11.

 14 I *révérence* right and curtsey left.

Repeat 12.

 15 My class has come to an end.

Press up onto the toes (*relevé*) with the legs together in first position. Take tiny steps on the toes (*bourrée*) while turning to the right. The arms are overhead in fifth position. Finish facing front again, coming down with feet flat. Open the arms to second position, then stretch to *allongé,* and then go back down to the *en bas* position.

A Fantasy Garden Ballet Class Part II

Center Floor Exercises

The exercises in this section are presented on the DVD *A Fantasy Garden Ballet Class II*
and on the music CD, *A Fantasy Garden Ballet Class Volume II*
bound inside the back cover of this book.

Emboîté Ants

Goals

Learning the terminology for and basic mechanics of *emboîté*.

Learning the terminology for and basic mechanics of *attitude*.

Increase aerobic activity.

Execute a movement at different speeds (slow and fast).

Strengthen legs and back.

Develop coordination, control and balance.

Learn diagonal spatial design.

Presentation and principles

Pretending to go up and down a hill helps the students execute the *emboîté* at different tempos and speeds.

Have students execute the *emboîté* at a slow tempo to develop coordination, control, and balance while strengthening the legs.

Make the students elongate their backs while jumping to increase their strength.

The lyrics reinforce the ballet terminology, *emboîté* and *attitude*, and the fact that the *emboîté* step uses the *attitude* positions.

Correcting common mistakes

Keep in time with the music on slower *emboîtés*.

Point toes while executing *emboîtés*.

Keep back tall and elongated while jumping.

Keep leg in attitude while jumping.

Advancement

Vary spatial designs.

The instrumental version of the music will challenge the students' musicality while they are executing *emboîtés* at the slower tempo.

Emboîté Ants

 1 This exercise teaches the student an *emboîté* **step. We lift the right leg to the front with the knee slightly bent (*attitude*). The toe is pointed and the standing leg is bent (*plié*). In this exercise we jump quickly from one foot to the other. We also do this slowly, stepping from one foot to the other.**

We do this exercise moving on the diagonal across the room. Here we are working with a partner. Begin feet together in parallel first position, hands on hips. Execute thirty-two *emboîtés* with the lyrics above, jumping quickly, in time with the music, remaining in place.

 2 The ants in the garden of fantasy work as hard as the other ants do. In fact they work even harder, because of the step they do. They *emboîté***, kicking their legs from** *attitude* **to** *attitude***, kicking all day, to the front.**

 3 Going up the hill is slow, it's such a long hard climb.

Begin moving forward diagonally, across the room, as you execute eight *emboîtés* slowly, stepping in time with the music.

 4 They put their food into the ant hole

Run to the center of the room and squat down (placing the food in the ant hole).

 5 Then come down, in a very short time.

Stand up and begin the *emboîtés* once more. Quickly move diagonally forward to the opposite corner of the room.

 6 The ants in the garden of fantasy keep busy all day long. They *emboîté* **and** *emboîté* **dancing to this song. They** *emboîté***, kicking their legs from** *attitude* **to** *attitude***. Kicking all day, to the front, from** *attitude* **to** *attitude***. Going up the hill is slow it's such a long hard climb. They put their food into the ant hole Then come down, in a very short time.**

The next group executes figures 2 through 5.

Note: There is no mention of spatial directions within the lyrics. In this case, we have shown the exercise being done on the diagonal with a partner. However, it can be done using different spatial designs with larger groups as well.

Mr. Robin Red Breast

Goals

Learn ballet walks (*pas marché*).

Articulate feet.

Develop musical sensitivity.

Stretch and strengthen legs.

Strengthen upper body and abdominals.

Learn *penché*, *arabesque* and *développé*.

Presentation and principles

The slow, calming music has an effect on the student's sensitivity to music. Movements should remain slow and fluid.

The imagery of moving quietly in the grass will influence the students to automatically lead with their toes as they walk.

Remind the students that they are moving slowly and have time to figure out the coordination needed to articulate their feet.

Placing the hands down on the floor stretches their hamstring muscles.

Correcting common mistakes

Use *plié* while walking.

Keep legs straight in *penché*.

Advancement

Vary spatial designs.

Switch to using the instrumental version of the music once the students know the exercise.

Mr. Robin Red Breast

 1 Mr. Robin Red Breast means spring is here at last. He's looking for some food

In this exercise we are moving straight across the room. Start feet together parallel in first position. The hands are on the hips. Extend the right foot forward with the toes pointed and the standing leg bent (*plié*). Then step onto the right leg placing the toes to the floor first. These are called ballet walks (*pas marché*). Repeat this with the left leg. This is done six times alternating feet, slowly, in time with the music.

 2 Beneath the green green grass

Take one more step forward with the right leg, then step feet together with the left, back to parallel first position.

 3 He puts his head down

Bend forward from the hips keeping feet together with legs straight. Place hands on the floor in front of you.

 4 Sticks his tail up. Pokes his beak into the earth

Lift the right foot up off the floor while bending the knee. Extend the right leg, reaching it up to the ceiling, with the leg straight and the toes pointed. The standing leg remains straight.

 5 Pulls out a worm

Bring the right leg back down to the floor to a squatting position, with hands on the floor in front. The head is tucked down.

 6 And gobbles him up

Stand up with legs straight and up on the toes (*relevé*). The feet are together, with the arms in fifth position overhead.

7 And flies up to his branch

Run on the toes (*bourrée*) to the end of the room. The arms flap like a bird.

8 To perch.

When you reach the end of the room, turn around, placing feet together in parallel first position with hands on the hips.
You are now ready to come back the other way, starting with the left leg this time.

Friendly Frogs

Goals

Strengthen legs.

Elevate with control.

Increase aerobic activity.

Improve coordination.

Elongate back while jumping.

Presentation and principles

Jumping from a squatting position will strengthen the legs.

This exercise should make repetition fun for the student.

The students develop coordination and learn how to open the legs into a wide second position while jumping.

Reaching the arms up and out creates an elongation of the spine while jumping.

The students learn to jump with control, having to land the jump in a specific place.

Correcting common mistakes

Control jumps.

Open legs while jumping.

Land with feet together.

Use upper body and arms to elongate back while jumping.

Advancement

Use the flower mats to vary spatial designs.

Once students have perfected their jumps, using maximum elevation and the coordination of a wide second position, you can have them jump over each other. They should take turns and work with a partner.

Friendly Frogs

 1 Students begin in a squatting position, in a line, with the hands on the floor, in front of them. Place seven mats *(see page 5)* **in front of them in a straight line touching each other. Here we have mats with lily pads painted on them.**

 2 There is a fantasy pond, with lily pads floating about.

The first student jumps up into the air, with the arms reaching out and up overhead. The legs reach out to the front as well. Keep them straight with the toes pointed. The student lands on the first lily pad mat in a squatting position.

 3 Where friendly frogs play all day, jumping and leaping about.

Repeat, landing on the second lily pad.

 4 They leap and jump carefully from one lily pad to another.

Repeat 2, landing on the third lily pad.

 5 They leap and jump carefully jumping over each other.

Repeat 2, landing on the fourth lily pad.

 6 Take a big leap over then squat and hold

Repeat 2, landing on the fifth lily pad.

 7 From one lily pad to another.

Repeat the jump landing on the sixth lily pad.

 8 And when they run out of lily pads, they jump right in the water.

Spot the student for a front roll–over. Make sure you tuck the student's head in, then carefully roll him or her over. When finished, each one gets up and runs back to the end of the line. The next student begins.

Leaping Ladybugs

Goals

Learn the terminology for and basic mechanics of *grand jeté*.

Use coordination and control while leaping.

Develop ankles and feet.

Increase aerobic activity.

Improve *port de bras*.

Presentation and Principles

The purpose of this exercise is to teach students that a leap is executed by jumping from one leg to the other. The song lyrics will reinforce the terminology.

Students will learn to control their leaps as they leap from one specific spot to another.

Running on the toes (*bourrée*) will help them develop strong ankles and feet.

We create an awareness of movement of the arms (*port de bras*) by imitating the motions of a ladybug's wings. The students work on coordination as they move their arms and feet simultaneously.

Correcting common mistakes

Leap from one leg.

Jump from two feet.

Leap with control.

Move arms continuously to develop the use of *port de bras* and coordination.

Advancement

Once the students have learned to control their leaps, have them leap all the way over their mats.

Leaping Lady Bugs

 This exercise can be done straight across the room or diagonally. Place a mat in the center of the room. The picture shows a mat painted like a flower *(see page 5)*.

1 Students stand in line and execute the exercise one at a time.

 2 Lady bugs, lady bugs, all around. Lady bugs, lady bugs, leaping

Run on the toes (*bourrée*) with the arms flapping like wings. Leap around the flower two times.

 3 off the ground.

Leap (*bourrée*) back to the line where you started. The wings are still flapping.

 4 They run on their toes as fast as they can and leap onto a flower.

Run on the toes (*bourrée*) and take a big leap on to the flower.

 5 Then turn on their toes and then leap down and run and find another.

Turn on the toes (*bourrée*) one time. Take a big leap off of the flower and run on the toes, with the wings still flapping, to the other side of the room. The next student in line repeats the exercise.

*Green Green
Galloping Grasshoppers*

Goals

Learn the terminology for and basic mechanics of gallop (*chassé*).

Successfully follow directional instruction.

Jump with elevation.

Presentation and principles

This exercise will refine the student's ability to execute the basic motor skill of galloping (*chassé*).

The students learn how to take directional instruction, having to gallop in a set pattern and direction around their mat.

The motivation of jumping up to scare someone causes the students to achieve maximum elevation on their jumps and full use of their legs and feet.

The students have fun reacting to each other and "scaring" each other.

Correcting common mistakes

Lead with the same leg when galloping (*chassé*).

Maintain gallop throughout exercise—no skipping or running!

Advancement

Instead of using one mat, place two or three around the room. Call the mats "rocks." Give children a more complicated pattern to follow as they travel to the rock (mat) to hide.

Green, Green, Galloping Grasshoppers

 1 Step out with the right foot to the front. Then jump in the air and bring the left foot together to the right foot. Land on the left foot and step out again with the right foot and repeat. The left leg can lead, as well. The basic movements of galloping are the same as the *chassé* in ballet.

 2 In the garden of fantasy the grasshoppers don't just hop, they gallop around the garden all day

This exercise is done moving across the room, working with a partner. Place an object in the middle of the room to represent a rock. We use a pile of our flower mats. The first student begins to gallop, as in 1, to the rock. Then he or she circles around the rock two times.

 3 And hide behind a rock.

The student then crouches down, as if to hide behind the imaginary rock.

 4 They gallop around the garden all day and hide behind a rock,

The next student gallops out to the rock.

 5 And when they see you coming, they hop up and give you a scare,

The first student jumps up from behind the rock. The second student jumps up as if startled.

 6 That's how the green, green, galloping grasshoppers, play all day, without a care.

The two students then take hands and gallop away to the other end of the room.

The Caterpillar Circle

Goals

Learn to work in a circular spatial design.

Improve musicality.

Strengthen legs, ankles and feet.

Successfully follow directional instruction.

Work together to create a spatial design.

Presentation and principles

Help students keep the circular design by having them hold hands and spread out while making the circle larger.

Encourage them to work together as circular directions are reinforced by everyone moving to the right or to the left at once.

Children learn the difference between facing in or out of the circle. They will learn to orient themselves on the circle as they move forward and backward.

Move in time to the music to develop musical sensitivity.

Changing levels while walking makes the students aware of their body shapes as they strengthen their legs, ankles and feet.

The students will learn to work together by holding hands while executing the upward and downward movements.

Correcting common mistakes

The students will initially have a difficult time grasping the concept of how to move the circle right and left. The easiest way to explain it to them is by having them turn to face the direction they will travel. Have them lead with their right hands to travel right and their left hands to travel left.

When holding hands on the upward and downward movements, the students will learn that they need to balance themselves individually throughout the movements. Remind them not to pull and tug on their fellow students.

Constantly work on making the upward and downward movements as big as possible.

Advancement

Change the directional instructions when facing inwardly and outwardly. One option is to have the students move the circle to the right when they face inward and to the left when they face outward.

The Caterpillar Circle

 Place an object in the middle of the floor to represent a purple flower. We have used a flower mat. Have the children make a big circle around the flower facing into the circle.

1 The feet are together in parallel first position, with hands on hips.

 2 A bunch of fuzzy caterpillars

Bend (*plié*) and straighten the knees two times, in time with the music.

 3 take hands and make a circle

Run into the circle, around the flower and take one another's hands.

 4 And do their caterpillar dance

Bend (*plié*) and straighten the knees two times in time with the music.

 5 Round their favorite flower of purple.

Turn to the right, still holding hands. The left shoulder will be facing into the circle.

 6 Up 2, 3

Take three steps, high up on the toes (*relevé*), moving forward, around in the circle in time with the music.

 7 Down 2, 3

Take three steps while crouched down low, continuing to move around in the circle.

 9 Down 2, 3, up 2, 3, down 2, 3 hold.

This is the same as 6 through 8, but in reverse. You begin down in the crouched position rather than up on the toes (*relevé*).

 10 Up 2, 3, down 2, 3, up 2, 3 hold.

This is a repeat of 6 through 8.

11 Then stay on their toes, and turn around, to face the outside

Begin to turn to the right around yourself, way up on the toes (*bourrée* turn). As you turn, begin to open up the whole circle, making it bigger. Turn as many times as needed. The arms are in fifth position overhead.

 12 Of the circle.

You will finish the turn facing the outside of the circle. The circle should now be big, the size of as the original circle as it was at the beginnning of the exercise.

 13 Yellow fuzzy caterpillars take hands and make a circle. And do their caterpillar dance, round their favorite flower of purple

The students now back up into the circle and hold hands facing the outside of the circle while executing the repeated movements 2 through 12.

Up 2, 3, down 2, 3,
up 2, 3, hold.
Down 2, 3, up 2, 3,
down 2, 3 hold.
Up 2, 3, down 2, 3,
up 2, 3 hold.

 Then stay on their toes and turn around and face the inside

Begin to turn right, around yourself, high up on the toes (*bourrée* turn). As you turn, begin to open up the circle, making it bigger. Turn as many times as needed. The arms are in fifth position overhead.

 Of the circle.

You finish the turn facing into the circle. The circle should be as big as it was when the exercise was started. The hands are on the hips with the feet together in parallel first position.

Prancing Petunias

Goals

Learn how to prance.

Strengthen legs, ankles and feet.

Learn to follow each other.

Use spatial design concepts creatively.

Develop sensitivity to music.

Increase aerobic activity.

Reinforce ability to use legs individually.

Presentation and principles

This exercise introduces prancing, one of the basic movements in dance. The *coupé* position is reinforced.

Encourage students to follow the song lyrics to reinforce proper use of legs while prancing. Paying attention to the lyrics will also help the students stay in time with the music.

Placing the mats randomly around the room, the leader can create his or her own spatial design while prancing around them. The other students learn to follow a pattern of direction that is not previously set.

Having to stop and start again to take a breath helps develop each student's sensitivity to the music. They should dance for three sets of eight counts and hold during the fourth set of eight counts.

Correcting common mistakes

Keep the foot pointed in *coupé*.

Hold the shape of the *coupé*, keeping foot against ankle

Prance in time to the music.

Advancement

Switch to using the instrumental version of the music once the students learn when to stop and start.

Prancing Petunias

This exercise teaches students how to prance.

1 Jumping from one foot to the other, place the foot on the ankle with toes pointed (*coupé*).

**2 Right and left, right and left, prancing like petunias.
Right and left, right and left, from one foot to the other.
Right and left, right and left, we stop and take a rest.
Getting ready to prance again, we take a big deep breath.**

This exercise has no specific spatial directions. It can be done in various ways. In the picture we are playing "follow the leader" while prancing through the flower mats. When the lyrics say **"take a big deep breath,"** the students stop and take a breath to rest.

Marching Marigolds

Goals

Refine the marching step.

Develop sense of rhythm.

Successfully follow one another.

Create personal spatial designs.

Successfully follow spatial instructions.

Increase aerobic activity.

Reinforce individual use of legs.

Presentation and principles

A marching step is relatively easy for students to comprehend. Since it is not a difficult movement, you are able to work on refining the step for use in dance. Work on the shape of a *passé*, holding the foot firmly against the knee.

Marching to the music and lyrics will develop musicality, rhythm and ability to differentiate between using the right or left leg.

Correcting common mistakes

Keep foot pointed in *passé*.

Keep foot on knee while in *passé*.

March in time to the music.

Advancement

Vary spatial designs. Let the students create their own spatial designs or ask them to create a certain design.

Marching Marigolds

This exercise can be done in many different ways, using various spatial directions and instructions. In this picture we have placed flowered mats around the room. The students play "follow the leader," while marching in time with the music. They are learning to march while picking up the knees and placing the foot on the supporting knee with the toes pointed (*passé*). This exercise will develop a sense of musicality and rhythm.

1 Right left right left, ready set and go
Beautiful blooming marigolds are marching in a row
Right left right left, ready set and go
Beautiful golden marigolds know how to point their toes.

2 They lift their petals up very, very, high
Reaching for the sun, way up in the sky.

3 Right, left, right, left, ready set and go
Beautiful blooming marigolds are marching in a row
Right, left, right, left, ready set and go
Beautiful golden marigolds know how to point their toes.

4 They lift their petals way up high, so I'm told
Because it is the sun that makes them beautiful and gold.

5 Repeat

6 Right, left, right, left, ready set and go
Beautiful blooming marigolds are marching in a row.

Coloring Pages for Students

Teachers may photocopy the following pages for their students to color.

The Sun

It's Morning

Butterfly

Mr. Inchworm

Big Oak Tree

Coupé the Cricket
(koo-pay)

Tendu the Tulip
(tahn-dew)

Port de bras
the Spider
(pawr-duh-brah)

Skippy the Squirrel

Chassé the Chipmunk
(sha-say)

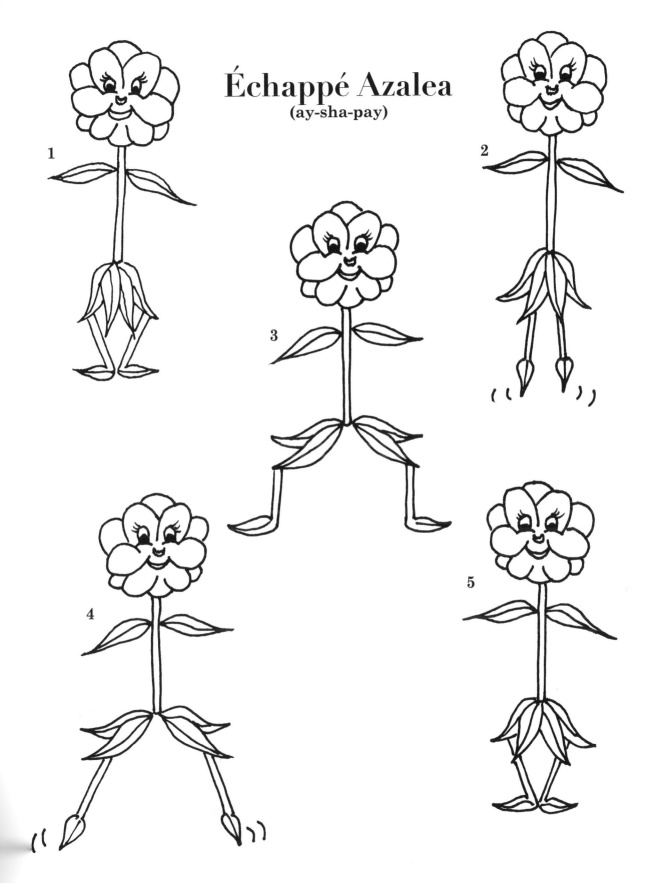

Échappé Azalea
(ay-sha-pay)

Bourrée the Bee
(boo-ray)

Sauté the Bunny

(soh-tay)

Pas de Chat the Pansy
(pah-duh-shah)

passé

passé

first

Plié the Poppy
(plee-ay)

Révérence
(ray-vay-rahnss)

Emboîté Ants
(em-bwa-tay)

Mr. Robin
Red Breast

Friendly Frogs

Leaping Ladybugs

Green, Green,
Galloping
Grasshoppers

The Caterpillar Circle

Prancing
Petunia

Marching Marigolds

Disk Programs

Concept and lyrics by Rosemary Boross
Music by Bruce Foster

A Fantasy Garden Ballet Class (Volume I)

1. The Sun (vocal)
2. The Sun (instrumental)
3. It's Morning (vocal)
4. It's Morning (instrumental)
5. Butterfly (vocal)
6. Butterfly (instrumental)
7. Mr. Inchworm (vocal)
8. Mr. Inchworm (instrumental)
9. Big Oak Tree (vocal)
10. Big Oak Tree (instrumental)
11. Tendu the Tulip (vocal)
12. Tendu the Tulip (instrumental)
13. Port de bras the Spider (vocal)
14. Port de bras the Spider (instrumental)
15. Skippy the Squirrel (front & back)
16. Skippy the Squirrel (right & left)
17. Skippy the Squirrel (instrumental)
18. Chassé the Chipmunk (1 clap)
19. Chassé the Chipmunk (2 claps)
20. Chassé the Chipmunk (3 claps)
21. Échappé Azalea (vocal)
22. Échappé Azalea (instrumental)
23. Coupé the Cricket (vocal)
24. Coupé the Cricket (instrumental)
25. Bourrée the Bee
26. Sauté the Bunny
27. Pas de chat the Pansy
28. Plié the Poppy
29. Creative Movement
30. Goodbye (Révérence) (vocal)
31. Goodbye (Révérence) (instrumental)

A Fantasy Garden Ballet Class (Volume II)

1. Emboîté Ants (vocal)
2. Emboîté Ants (instrumental)
3. Mr. Robin Red Breast (vocal)
4. Mr. Robin Red Breast (instrumental)
5. Friendly Frogs (vocal)
6. Friendly Frogs (instrumental)
7. Leaping Lady Bugs (vocal)
8. Leaping Lady Bugs (instrumental)
9. Marching Marigolds (vocal)
10. Marching Marigolds (instrumental)
11. Green Galloping Grasshoppers (vocal)
12. Green Galloping Grasshoppers (instrumental)
13. The Caterpillar Circle (vocal)
14. The Caterpillar Circle (instrumental)
15. Prancing Petunias (vocal)
16. Prancing Petunias (instrumental)